The Power

of a

Woman

Dr. Cassundra White-Elliott

Published by CLF PUBLISHING, LLC. 3281 E. Guasti Road, Seventh Floor, Ontario, CA 91761.
(760) 669-8149.

Cover Design by Senir Design. Contact information- info@senirdesign.com.

ISBN # 978-0-9899408-0-1

Printed in the United States of America.

Dedications

This book is dedicated to all the women who told me I have power (and some told me how to operate in it):

Gloria L. Harrison, my mother (deceased)

Mildred M. Williams, my grandmother (deceased)

Julia L. Lary, my aunt

Quantanique S. Williams, my niece

Octavia A. Manning-Miller, my goddaughter

and

All the women of God who have spoken into my life

Acknowledgements

I acknowledge every person who came to test my physical strength, my faith, and my mental acuity. I say to you all, "God is yet on the throne, and He is yet doing wonders in my life."

Table of Contents

Introduction

From biblical times to the present day, men and women alike have debated women's position in the world. At times, women have been held back from reaching their full potential, while at other times, they have had more freedom to progress and excel. Overall, women have struggled to be seen as equal with men. Men, as well as women, have questioned women's worth. Women have been seen as inferior to men. The list of disparities and contrasts between men and women is long. However, God never intended this struggle to exist. Women were never expected to have to prove their equality. Rather, God created men and women to be equals, with man as the head of woman. Man's headship in no way demeans woman, but unfortunately, God's plan has been skewed, misinterpreted and negatively altered. As a result, women have been misused and abused.

This book will shed light on the woman's position in the earth realm from God's perspective and according to His divine plan. As you read, read with an open mind. Although a woman wrote this book, it honestly shares God's perspectives about women and not solely the perspectives of the author. The author, Dr. Cassundra

White-Elliott is just a mouthpiece, a vessel used of God to share this message to women and men alike.

1

God's Uniquely Designed Creation- The Woman

To effectively articulate the function of God's unique and necessary design- woman, I must first begin with a descriptive detailed account of the creation of the *first* human- man. To do this accurately, I will draw all facts from the word of God, specifically from the book of Genesis. Genesis, the first book of the Bible, is a story of beginnings and includes a lot of 'firsts.' However, our focus is on the *first* human- man and then on the second human- woman. Once the accounts of the creation of man and then woman have been descriptively explained, correlations, as well as comparisons and contrasts, can be drawn with the sole purpose of demonstrating God's uniquely designed creation- woman and her function in the earth realm.

Genesis Chapter 1, Verse 26 states, "*Then God said, 'Let us make man in our image...*'" Verse 27 continues, "*So God created man in his own image*" (Quest Bible New International Version (NIV)). Notice in the first chapter of Genesis, man's creation is mentioned very succinctly. We are simply told that man *was* made, but the details have been excluded. To understand the detailed account of the creation of man, we must carefully peruse Genesis Chapter 2.

Prior to the creation of man, God created the heavens, the earth, land vegetation, sea creatures, fowl of the air, and all animals. After these tasks were completed, God saw there was not anyone to cultivate the earth. So, He formed man. Genesis 2:7 states, *"Then the Lord God formed the man from the dust of the ground. He breathed..."* (Quest Bible NIV). After man was created and had come alive with the breath of life that quickened his mortal body, God placed him in the Garden of Eden to tend it and to watch over it (V. 15).

While Adam was on duty in the garden and enjoying all of God's creation, he was also tasked with naming all the livestock, birds, and wild animals (V. 20, Tyndale New Living Translation (NLT)). Being astute, as he was formed in God's image, Adam took note as he was naming the animals that something about them was different from himself: All animal forms had representation of both sexes- male and female. But for the one human, that was not the case.

Verses 21 and 24, of the first chapter, make the fact that both sexes existed readily apparent. These two verses state the sea creatures, every bird, livestock, small animals and wild animals were to produce offspring after their own kind. All of us have lived long enough to know procreation can only occur between a male and a female of the same kind (unless, of course, God made them to function otherwise). When both a male and female of the same species fail to exist, the species becomes extinct.

As Adam watched the animals interact with each other, it became very apparent to him that there was not another creature like him. He did not have a suitable counterpart. There was no one with whom he could procreate.

But God was not yet finished with creation! Creation at that point was incomplete. But there was still time left, as it was only day six. The heavens, the earth, stars, firmament, land, water, fowl, fish, animals, vegetation, and man had all been created and all were present. However, the one who would be ultimately responsible for birthing the furtherance of mankind was not yet on the scene. Because of the great tasks that lay ahead of woman, God viewed it as necessary that she be uniquely created. Because of her impending position as partner and helper of man, it was deemed necessary that God use a special one-time process to create woman. To ensure she would not forever be belittled, viewed as a second-class citizen, or treated as less than worthy, God had to create her in a manner that no other creation was created. The very process deemed her as unique.

Thus, the first surgery ensued!

In the preparatory stages of this one-time type of surgery, to form a creation to be treasured, respected, and loved, God caused Adam to fall into a deep sleep. As the great anesthesiologist (who needed no chemicals), God anesthetized Adam, so he would feel no pain. While Adam was asleep, God carefully and craftily made an incision in Adam's side. After opening up Adam's side, God removed one of Adam's ribs and some of his flesh.

Genesis 2:22a states, "Then the Lord made a woman from the rib (Tyndale NLT). With this statement, many readers assume God fashioned the woman with *only* one of Adam's ribs, and nothing more. However, once Adam awoke from the deep sleep, he was able to witness the brilliant creation God had formed. Upon seeing the woman, Adam spoke saying, *"This is now bone of my bone and flesh of my flesh"* (V. 23). Adam's statement demonstrates God's use of both Adam's bone and flesh in the creation of Eve.

From the hard, strong, sturdy rib and the soft, supple flesh, God fashioned a creature, who has the same elements within her being. A woman is strong enough to bear children, teach and train them, and bring them up in the admonition of the Lord. She has the strength to stand by her man in the midst of adversity, endure hardship and heartbreak, and be a shoulder for him when he is facing trials and needs a support system. At the same time, a woman is soft and gentle. She is a nurturer. She is a mother. She is a counselor. She is a teacher, a nurse, a cook, a seamstress, and a talebearer. She can be all things to her family and change roles when needed. She is malleable and not rigid. She is patient, loving, kind, and understanding.

Looking once again at the biblical account, for all of God's creations, you will find the creation of woman very unique indeed. Genesis 1:24 states, *"Then God said, 'Let the earth produce every sort of animal'"* (Tyndale NLT). This means all creatures were created from the dust of the ground. Let me reiterate, all the animals and the first man were created from the dust of the ground. When God formed Adam from the dust, He could have easily fashioned Eve from the dust right beside Adam. However, He did not. There are many reasons why God created woman in the manner He did. Many of these reasons will be explored in the coming chapters.

For now women, know this- you were uniquely designed by God Himself in a manner that no other creation was- as a result of a one-time surgery. With that one fact in mind, you should recognize you are special and you have purpose.

To further exemplify the unique design of woman and her necessity in the earth realm, we need to examine the circumstances that led to her existence. Let us look closely at the words God spoke prior to her creation. In Genesis 2:18, God is recorded as saying, *"It is not good for man to be alone. I will make a helper who is just right for him"* (Tyndale NLT).

The phrase "It is not good" signifies a great contrast to what God had observed repeatedly prior to that point, during His early stages of creation. In the following verses, notice the contrast. The same phrase of acceptance/approval was recorded in Chapter 1:4, 10, 12, 18, 21, and 25. These verses illustrate how God saw six times that His creation 'was good.' He was pleased with what He saw. That is- until He saw Adam alone, without a counterpart. However, after Eve was created, God looked back at all He had created- the heavens; the earth; the fish of the sea; the fowl of the air; the rivers, lakes, seas, and oceans; the livestock and wild animals; the stars, the sun, and the moon; the wind and the rain; the seasons; man and woman- and His impression changed. He no longer approved with 'it is good' and he no longer disapproved with 'it is not good.' Rather, He looked, and He saw that it was *very* good (Genesis 1:31, Tyndale NLT). God's creation had been completed with the creation of woman. Man then had a suitable counterpart, one with whom he could procreate, to replenish the earth.

Women, we, like men, were created in God's image. Genesis 1:27 says, *"So God created mankind in his own image, in the image of God he created them; male and female he created them"* (biblegateway.com/NIV). We were not an afterthought, and we did **not** originally only have one purpose. God's purposes for woman are multifaceted. Read the next chapter for more detail.

2

Know Your Worth
(From God's Perspective)

Throughout history, from the creation of Adam and Eve to today's time, women have been, and at times still are, viewed to be inferior to men. Contrary to this belief, Galatians 3:28 states, *"There is neither Jew nor Gentiles, neither slave nor free, nor is there male and female, for you are all one in Christ Jesus."* Under the law of Moses, Jews were seen as superior to any other race, men were superior to women (due to their circumcised condition), and free individuals were superior to slaves. However, after the shedding of Christ's blood and the fact that believers are now saved by grace and not the law, old things, such as 'the law,' have passed away. 2 Corinthians 5:17 says, *"Therefore, if anyone is in Christ, the new creation has come. The old has gone, the new is here!"* (biblegateway.com/NIV). In Christ, all people have equal status.

Now, you may be thinking- all the people on earth do not belong to God because all people have not accepted Christ as their Lord and Savior. And you may be asking, "How does this impact men and women's status of equality?" Their religious standing is of no consequence because Psalm 24:1 states, *"The earth is the LORD's, and everything in it, the world, and all who live in it"* (bible.cc.com/NIV). So whether or not man believes males are superior to females, God does not share this perspective, and it is His perspective that matters. And, God will have the final say!

Even with the biblical perspective documented for everyone to see, we know that the world system operates according to its own terms, needs, and desires; basically, the selfish desires of humans and their twisted viewpoints are at work, and the word of God is ignored by many. This is primarily due to the powers of the devil. Ephesians 2:2 states, *"You used to live in sin, just like the rest of the world, obeying the devil--the commander of the powers in the unseen world. He is the spirit at work in the hearts of those who refuse to obey God"* (bible.cc.com/NLT).

Unfortunately, in addition to unbelievers who work Satan's plan, there are some believers who still operate under the influences of the world system. They have not permitted the words of the Lord in 2 Corinthians 5:17 to penetrate their being.

The History of Women in America

Let us, for a moment, take a look at the history of women in the United States to view the full impact of the negative view of women on society. Although the negativity began during biblical times, it was not exempt from occurring in other eras. As we take a look into history, we will see the progression of liberality for women as they are more often seen as equal to men by the society in which they reside. At the same time, we will take note of the degradation women have suffered and continue to suffer.

To begin, U.S. history indicates women had fewer legal rights and employment opportunities. From long ago, women were viewed only suitable for child bearing, child rearing, being wives, and for domestic chores. Today, this view is still held by not only some men, but by many women also, especially older women and is expressed openly.

For example, if a group of married women of various ages are sitting around a table discussing their careers and responsibilities, sooner or later someone will ask the question, "Do you cook dinner for your husband?" Whether or not the women cook dinner for their husbands is of no significance or regard to me. What I find interesting is the amount of importance that is placed upon who is taking the responsibility of the household chores. For many, it does not matter if a woman works as many hours as a man, or if she contributes to the financial stability of the household. The thought is- she should still be solely responsible for the well-being of the home. To me, this type of thinking keeps women in positions of old. How can women progress if other women, along with men, hold these debilitating viewpoints?

In today's age, it usually takes two working parents to have a financially stable home. If both parents work a full-time job, is it fair to require the wife to go home and work another 20-30-40 hours a week while the husband sits back and kicks his feet up and watches a football game? There must be balance.

However, there are those who do not see it that way. They believe cooking and cleaning are women's work. And, if a woman is not cooking, cleaning, and caring for the children, she is deemed a bad wife.

Please note- by no means am I advocating for women to neglect any responsibilities she and her husband have agreed she will be responsible for. My point is- the husband and wife should agree on who is going to do what in their home. Outside influences should stay exactly there- outside!

The Education of Women

Because women were trained as young girls to be wives and mothers, their academic achievement suffered. Typically, when a young girl began school, she was very excited and her intellectual prowess was illustrated. However, at home, a girl's training for her future superseded her school work. Thus, somewhere along the way, it became clear she was only expected to have a future as a wife and mother. As these thoughts penetrated the young girl's mind, she saw her own education as unnecessary because she was not on a career path. With this realization, the girl's grades began to decrease and her enthusiasm towards school diminished.

This, of course, was not indicative of all young girls. It really depended upon what her parents and teachers were speaking into her life. But in the days of old- bible times up to the early 1900s- women were primarily trained to be housewives. In the early 1900s, this stereotypical view of women began to give way to the innermost desires women were experiencing. Women, like men, had dreams and desires. They no longer looked forward to the confines of their homes. As a result, girls began to be trained a little differently. They were still taught how to cook, clean, and raise children. However, they were encouraged to excel in school and to choose a career path if they so desired. Formal education for girls was no longer secondary to the education boys received. Girls no longer only attended school if there was room after the boys enrolled.

By the end of the nineteenth century, the number of women students had greatly increased (Women's History in America (WHA), 1994). At the beginning of the twentieth century, women accounted for 19% of all undergraduate degrees (WHA, 1994). That number increased to 49% by the mid-1980s (WHA, 1994).

Women in the Workforce

With the rise of educated women, the number of women in the workforce drastically increased. However, the primary suitable jobs for women were as writers and teachers. Very few women were doctors and lawyers. Many women were involved in obstetrics, but they did not work in hospitals; they worked in the home, as midwives. The medical profession consisted almost exclusively of men. The American Medical Association (AMA) actually barred women from membership from 1846 to 1915 (WHA, 1994). Eventually, entrance to the AMA was granted to women who had completed medical school. Most women were only able to complete medical school because they had formed their own medical school for women, as they were not permitted to attend the presently formed medical schools that were strictly for men.

By 1890, 5% of the doctors were women, and this number has increased decade by decade. The same is true for the increase in women lawyers, dentists, engineers, etc. Regardless of these increases, the majority of women still serve as teachers, nurses, secretaries, waitresses, housecleaners, hairdressers, retail salespersons, bookkeepers, machine operators, etc.

With the increase of the number of women in these varied positions that at one time were only open to men, an increase in pay has also been seen. At one time, men and women were not paid equally for the same job. In 1963, the Equal Pay Act was passed. This Act did not automatically institute equal pay, however. But as time progressed, women began to see increased pay rates (WHA, 1994).

Women's Legal Status

Not only did the belief that women are inferior to men impact women's educational and employment status, it also impacted their legal status. In the early development of the U.S., women were the property of their husbands; as a result, women had no voice (WHA, 1994). However, the Equity Law, which originated in Europe and whose effects trickled over to the U.S., recognized equal rights between men and women, thereby overruling tradition and making such customs outdated. This, of course, did not grant immediate change.

By 1854, married women became able to own property separately from their husbands. By 1963, the Equal Pay Act passed enabling women to earn equal wages as men. In 1964, the Civil Rights Act was passed and prohibited discrimination against women by any company with 25 or more employees.

Women as Sex Symbols/Human Trafficking

Women have been projected as sex symbols even before the advent of media. Today, we see sex symbols everywhere, from the newspaper, to magazines, to television shows, movies, commercials, and even on the Internet. Models were typically 5'7"-5'9," thin, Caucasian, and blonde. However, as time progressed, models with dark hair began to be used, but all else remained the same. In addition to being tall and thin, the women usually have large breasts that attract men. Moving forward in time, various shades of women began to be seen in advertisements. Just recently, full-figure women have been seen in ads. But, regardless of the size, shape, or complexion of the women who have been included in the media, women have still been presented as sex symbols. For example, in beer commercials, the women wear tight t-shirts, short shorts, etc. This plain and simple is exploitation of women.

This type of exploitation leads to more mistreatment of women as it relates to sex. Prostitution is known as the world's oldest profession. When women were not permitted in the workforce, they found ways to make money. Some women worked as prostitutes by choice while other women were forced to have sex with strange men for money. Today, prostitution is still going on worldwide where women sell themselves to men and other women, and men sell themselves to women and other men. Not only are adults (18 and up) selling their bodies, but teenagers are involved in prostitution as well.

With sex being an everyday occurrence, it is high on the list of things sought after. To fulfill people's urges and fleshly desires, human trafficking is at an all-time high. According to the United Nations Office of Drugs and Crime, human trafficking is defined as, "the acquisition of people by improper means, such as force, fraud or deception, with the aim of exploiting them" (Archer, 2013). Trafficking is done in many forms, with the most explicit being sexual.

The monetary gain of trafficking is estimated at $32 billion per year and is the second largest crime industry in the world (Archer, 2013).

A Woman's Worth

With everything that has taken place in our world and with everything that continues to take place, it is no wonder females (from older women to young girls) have a skewed vision of who they are or can be. From being treated as second-class citizens to being used for sexual pleasure, women have felt worthless, belittled and meaningless. However, this frame of thought could not be further from the truth.

Remember, women, like men, were created in the image of God Himself. He is not to be degraded, belittled, chastised, etc. Therefore, women should not be either. Going back to the creation of woman in Chapter 1 of this book, you will recall Eve was created from a rib that was extracted from Adam. Notice the placement of the ribs within the human body. They are located on both our sides. Obviously, God was set upon using one of Adam's bones to fashion Eve. Was He required to use a rib? Of course not. He could have used a bone from Adam's skull. He could have used a bone from Adam's foot. He could have used a bone from Adam's tailbone. Or, He could have used a bone from Adam's sternum, which is located in the center of the front of the chest.

However, God chose the rib due to its placement. A bone from the foot would indicate an inferior position for women. A bone from the skull would indicate a superior position to man. A bone from the front of man would indicate a position of leadership for the woman. A bone from the back of man would indicate the woman's subservient position to man. The rib, however, indicates a position of equality for women. It indicates man and woman are to walk side by side. At the same time, we know that man is the head of his wife as Christ is the head of the church. God has order, and order must be adhered to. Note- headship does not mean dictatorship. Headship also does not mean superiority. Headship simply is a position of authority.

God's View of Women

To further assist women with their identity crisis, self-image and self-worth, let us go again to the word of God. Proverbs 23:7a states, *"For as a man thinketh in his heart, so is he"* (bible.cc.com/ King James Version (KJV)). This verse tells us what we think about ourselves is what we will be. Leaving this as a blanket statement can cause problems for some if they are not sober minded. So, let me provide you with another scripture that may prevent pitfalls in your thinking.

Romans 12:3 warns us, *"For by the grace (unmerited favor of God) given to me I warn everyone among you not to estimate and think of himself more highly than he ought [not to have an exaggerated opinion of his own importance], but to rate his ability with **sober** judgment, each according to the degree of faith apportioned by God to him"* (biblegateway.com/AMP (Amplified Bible)). This verse plainly tells us that we must know exactly who God created us to be. We are not to elevate ourselves and think more highly of ourselves. Here, we are warned against the spirit of pride, which has been many men's downfall. At the same time, we must be equally as careful to not demote ourselves. Demoting one's self can cause one to suffer from low self-esteem. To think soberly means to use proper judgment.

With that in mind, we as women should see ourselves as God sees us. We should recognize why He created us and understand we have value and we have purpose. We are not second-class citizens; we are not subservient to men; we are not on earth to be used and abused; we have purpose and with that we have a voice.

Using Your Voice Properly

Women, just because God has given us a voice does not mean we have the right to abuse the privilege. Remember, *"A soft answer turns away wrath, but a harsh word stirs up anger"* (Proverbs 15:1, New King James Version (NKJV), biblegateway.com). Therefore, it is really important that we know how to use our voices. We should know when to speak in a soft, loving tone and when we need to use a stern voice. This depends solely upon to whom we are speaking and the situation. For example, if we are training our children, we should use encouraging words with a loving tone. If we are disciplining our children, we may use stern words, but with a loving tone. When we speak to our husbands, we should use a tone of respect. Each situation will dictate our tone, our choice of words, and our voice level. Most importantly, we are not to abuse our power by using the improper voice type.

Jesus' Interaction with Women

To further illustrate how God views women, let us examine God's use of women in the Bible. From our Lord and Savior Jesus Christ, we obtain a true account of how God views women. Jesus came to earth in bodily form clothed with flesh. To enter into this world system, God the Father, deemed it necessary that Christ be born of a woman, as all other mankind is and was, with the exception of Adam and Eve. The first man may have not entered the world via the womb of a woman, but the most important man to mankind did. This illustrates the worth and necessity of a woman.

As it relates to social conventions and the status quo in regards to women, Jesus set His own rules and His own standards. When no one would be seen speaking to an adulteress woman in public, Jesus was. In John 8:2-11, the following account is shared:

> At dawn he appeared again in the temple courts, where all the people gathered around him, and he sat down to teach them. The teachers of the law and the Pharisees brought in a woman caught in adultery. They made her stand before the group and said to Jesus, 'Teacher, this woman was caught in the act of adultery. In the Law Moses commanded us to stone such women. Now what do you say?' They were using this question as a trap, in order to have a basis for accusing him. But Jesus bent down and started to write on the ground with his finger. When they kept on questioning him, he straightened up and said to them, 'Let any one of you who is without sin be the first to throw a stone at her.' Again he stooped down and wrote on the ground. At this, those who heard began to go away one at a time, the older ones first, until only Jesus was left, with the woman still standing there. Jesus straightened up and asked her, 'Woman, where are they? Has no one condemned you?' 'No one, sir,' she said. 'Then neither do I condemn you,' Jesus declared. 'Go now and leave your life of sin.' (biblegateway.com/NIV)

In this passage, Jesus is in the temple and is focused on teaching the Word of God. In the midst of His session, the lawmakers and Pharisees interrupt the time of study and fellowship to tie up Jesus' time with a matter they obviously deemed more important: adultery. Note this-from the time the first adulterous act was committed until the time the very last adulterous act will be committed in the future, the act has always included and will always include at least two persons. However, the lawmakers and the Pharisees only brought one guilty party to Jesus for sentencing. Where was the other party and why wasn't he standing accused as the woman was? This question has been asked time and time again, and I'm sure many have attempted to answer this query. But, our focus is not on what the male accusers did, but it is on what Jesus did.

In the midst of all of this confusion, the woman was probably frightened as she waited to be judged by Jesus. Undoubtedly, she expected further words of condemnation to be spoken by this man whom she stood before. However, Jesus remained calm. As the snare lay before His feet waiting to entrap Him, He focused on the words He spoke aloud and the words He wrote on the ground. Once the crowd had dispersed, Jesus, remaining composed, calmly spoke to the woman. When He spoke, He was alone with her. This, however, did not bother Him in the least. He did not hurriedly dismiss the woman. He did not try to make a quick exist. He did not purport to be better than she was. He simply told her He would not accuse her, and He told her to leave her past in the past.

Look at how unique Jesus' actions and words were. He was confident and secure within Himself that He did not allow the rumors to sway Him or determine His actions toward the accused woman.

In Jesus' time, many were accused. In our time, many are accused. Ecclesiastes 1:9 says there is nothing new under the sun. If that is true, why do we continue to allow ourselves to be shocked when one of us is accused? Don't you know that Satan is an accuser of the brethren (Revelation 12:10)? He comes to steal, kill, and destroy our reputations. We can be used of Satan like the lawmakers and Pharisees who were out to hurt the woman and Jesus. Or, we can stand our ground as Jesus did and band together and protect one another. I Peter 4:8 says, *"Above all, love each other deeply, because love covers over a multitude of sins"* (NIV). Jesus did not condemn the woman. Instead, He showed love toward her.

Women and men alike need to stand by one another. We need to pull one another up when we are down instead of taking the opportunity to crush someone further or step on the person's neck to ostracize him/her. We need to be loving and forgiving towards one another. In this, we all will find strength to be better people.

When no one would speak to the Samaritan woman who was a half-breed (half Jew and half Assyrian) and had had five husbands, Jesus did. In John Chapter 4, we read of Jesus taking an opportunity to minister one-on-one with a Samaritan woman. This account is particularly important for several reasons, but namely because it demonstrates what Jesus did was done from His heart. He did not do it for the purpose of being seen and noticed by a crowd. He conversed with the woman for one purpose and one purpose only: to save her soul.

As we delve into this passage of Scripture, we must first consider this- nothing in Jesus' life occurred by happenstance (Jackson, 2013). Every move He made was divinely orchestrated by God to lead Him to the cross and touch lives on the way. At that point in Jesus' ministry, His popularity had caused great strife among the Jewish leaders. If Jesus had fallen into their hands before the appointed, pre-ordained time, all would not have gone according to God's schedule. So, Jesus detoured through Samaria to keep His divine appointment with the Samaritan woman who was in no way expecting Him.

As Jesus passed through Samaria, He came upon Jacob's well. While He was stopped, due to His exhausted condition, a Samaritan woman approached the well to draw water. At that time, although Jesus had been with some of His disciples, He was alone, for they had *"gone into the city to buy food"* (John 4:8, New American Standard Bible (NASB)). Jesus with His calm demeanor said, *"Give me to drink"* (John 4:7, KJV). Jesus' request caused the woman to be totally taken aback. With His utterance, He broke social and cultural rules.

First, it was not customary for Jewish men to speak to women in public. This tradition did not refer only to strange woman, but to female family members as well. Second, Jews did not converse with Samaritans- male or female. But here, we have Jesus who is openly speaking to a Samaritan woman. What could He have possible been thinking? Obviously, it did not matter to Him what her sex was. Also, it obviously did not matter to Him her cultural background. What was predominant in the Lord's mind was she was and would continue to be a lost soul unless she came into the knowledge of the truth. So, with this thought, Jesus spoke and did not allow the negative impact and stigmas of society to cause Him to refrain from saving a soul.

After requesting a drink of water, the conversation between Jesus and the woman developed further, and He told her about the "living water" He could give her that would disable her thirst. This woman had a thirst for men. She had had five husbands prior and was currently with another man whom she was not currently married to. Jesus told her plainly and simply, if she were to drink from the living water, she would no longer continue to seek in such an unhealthy manner. This, of course, was His implied message.

Many times when we are presented with opportunities to minister, we let the moments roll right past us. This sometimes is due to what is socially acceptable and what is not. Instead of focusing on the society man has created, we need to focus on what is pleasing and acceptable to God. Would God want us to sacrifice someone's soul because his/her position is socially unacceptable? Of course not! Jesus' actions should be a lesson to us to care more about the soul than the earthly status a person holds.

In demonstrating the necessity of persistent prayer, while others may refrain from or be hesitant to use women as examples of persistence, such as the woman who was unrelenting with the unjust judge, Jesus did not refrain or hesitate. Luke 18:1-8 shares the following parable:

> *And he told them a parable to show that they must always pray and not be discouraged, saying, 'There was a certain judge in a certain town who did not fear God and did not respect people. And there was a widow in that town, and she kept coming to him, saying, "Grant*

me justice against my adversary!" And he was not willing for a time, but after these things he said to himself, "Even if I do not fear God or respect people, yet because this widow is causing trouble for me, I will grant her justice, so that she does not wear me down in the end by her coming back!" And the Lord said, 'Listen to what the unrighteous judge is saying! And will not God surely see to it that justice is done to his chosen ones who cry out to him day and night, and will he delay toward them? I tell you that he will see to it that justice is done for them soon! Nevertheless, when the Son of Man comes, then will he find faith on earth?' (biblegateway.com/LEB (Lexham English Bible))

There were probably other examples of persistent prayer Jesus could have used to illustrate His point. However, He used the one of this particular woman. Others may have deemed her to be a nag, but Jesus viewed her actions of persistence as necessary.

This example demonstrates to us that it is okay to use our voices in our times of trouble and in our times of need. Our society teaches us women should be silent. We should be seen only and not heard. We should allow our husbands to speak for us. But this woman was a widow. Who was going to speak on her behalf? What are the single women and widows of today supposed to do? According to Jesus' parable, women are to use the voices God has supplied them with to make their requests known (Philippians 4:6).

People are afraid to allow those rumored to be unclean to touch them, such as the woman who washed Jesus' feet with her hair and poured expensive cologne upon them, but Jesus did. And, He did it in public at the house of the

Pharisee who had invited Him to dinner. Read the full
account of Luke 7:36-50:

*When one of the Pharisees invited Jesus to have dinner
with him, he went to the Pharisee's house and reclined
at the table. A woman in that town who lived a sinful life
learned that Jesus was eating at the Pharisee's house, so
she came there with an alabaster jar of perfume. As she
stood behind him at his feet weeping, she began to wet
his feet with her tears. Then she wiped them with her
hair, kissed them and poured perfume on them. When
the Pharisee who had invited him saw this, he said to
himself, 'If this man were a prophet, he would know who
is touching him and what kind of woman she is—that
she is a sinner.' Jesus answered him, 'Simon, I have
something to tell you.' 'Tell me, teacher,' he said. 'Two
people owed money to a certain moneylender. One owed
him five hundred denarii, and the other fifty. Neither of
them had the money to pay him back, so he forgave the
debts of both. Now which of them will love him more?'
Simon replied, 'I suppose the one who had the bigger
debt forgiven.' 'You have judged correctly,' Jesus said.
Then he turned toward the woman and said to Simon,
'Do you see this woman? I came into your house. You did
not give me any water for my feet, but she wet my feet
with her tears and wiped them with her hair. You did not
give me a kiss, but this woman, from the time I entered,
has not stopped kissing my feet. You did not put oil on
my head, but she has poured perfume on my feet.
Therefore, I tell you, her many sins have been forgiven—
as her great love has shown. But whoever has been
forgiven little loves little.' Then Jesus said to her, 'Your
sins are forgiven.' The other guests began to say among
themselves, 'Who is this who even forgives sins?' Jesus*

said to the woman, 'Your faith has saved you; go in peace.' (biblegateway.com/NIV)

There are many lessons that can be taught and learned from Jesus' experience with this particular woman. The one we will focus on is the lesson of creating a negative reputation for oneself. Let us focus our attention on Verse 39, which states, *"When the Pharisee who had invited him saw this, he said to himself, 'If this man were a prophet, he would know who is touching him and what kind of woman she is—that she is a sinner.'"* Because Jesus allowed the woman to touch Him, His identity was now being called into question. At the time of this occurrence, Jesus had already become known as one who could foretell events. So, when the Pharisee made the statement in Verse 39 about whether or not Jesus was a prophet, he wasn't sincerely questioning Jesus' identity. Instead, he was being sarcastic about this man who allowed the unclean woman to touch Him.

After the Pharisee's sarcastic statement, Jesus calmly explained the difference between the actions of the host and the actions of the woman (Verses 44-46). He demonstrated how the woman's actions were indicative of the love she had for Christ.

Like the Pharisee in this passage, we often avoid people who carry negative reputations because we do not want our reputations to be tarnished by our involvement with them. However, our involvement may shed a different light upon who the person actually is. From the woman's actions in this passage of scripture, we can clearly see one's character and level of integrity is not always synonymous with one's reputation.

Jesus even permitted the woman who had the issue of blood to touch the hem of His garment, but many of us- men and women alike- would have shied away from her. Luke 8:43-48 shares the incident of the miraculous healing of the woman who bore the issue of blood for twelve years. She was convinced of Jesus' healing virtue and was determined to get as close to Him as possible. Seeing how congested the crowd was and realizing how low the odds were to actually have direct interaction with Jesus, she reasoned if she could just touch the hem of his garment, she would receive her healing. At the moment of her touch, Jesus felt differently and said, *"But Jesus said, "Someone touched me; I know that power has gone out from me"* (V. 46).

Those who heard Jesus' statement probably thought it was ridiculous for Him to declare someone touched Him, for He *was* in the midst of a crowd. It is quite expected to be touched by several persons when walking through a crowd. But it wasn't the mere touching that concerned Jesus. It was the result of the touching that had His attention. He wanted to know the distinct purpose of the touch and the result. Verse 47 provides a response to Jesus' statement as the woman came forth and publicly described what she had endured for twelve years and her miraculous healing.

Instead of being concerned with the physical condition of the person who may come near enough to us to touch us, we should be concerned about why he/she wants to touch us. We should ask ourselves, "What do I have to offer that may be beneficial to someone?" If we find we have nothing to offer to another, we should be concerned about that.

The term 'the women' we constantly see in the Bible as we read of Jesus' earthly ministry referred to His female disciples who stood by Him faithfully. These women led to the first evangelist who was A WOMAN!

God has purpose for us women!

3

Know Your Function
(Using Your God-Given Abilities)

In Romans 12:3, Apostle Paul wrote, *"For I say, through the grace given unto me, to every man that is among you, not to think of himself more highly than he ought to think; but to think soberly, according as God hath dealt to every man the measure of faith."*

In our society, and even among believers, we have a tendency to have a misconception of who we as individuals are. Some of us have the spirit of low self esteem, while others have the spirit of pride. Both of these spirits are contrary to the spirit of God that should live in us and speak to us- telling us exactly who we are.

Apostle Paul tells us in the above scripture that we are responsible for knowing exactly who we are. We are not to think any more highly of ourselves *or* lower of ourselves than we are.

Psalms 8:3-9 says,

When I consider thy heavens, the work of thy fingers, the moon and the stars, which thou hast ordained; What is man, that thou art mindful of him? and the son of man, that thou visitest him? For thou hast made him a little lower than the angels, and hast crowned him with glory and honour. Thou madest him to have dominion over the works of thy hands; thou hast put all things under his feet: All sheep and oxen, yea, and the beasts of the field; The fowl of the air, and the fish of the sea, and whatsoever passeth through the paths of the seas. O Lord our Lord, how excellent is thy name in all the earth!

God thinks highly of us. His positioning of us over all His creation tells us that. We are positioned just lower than the angels, those whom God keeps in His divine company. Rejoice in knowing how special and valuable we are to the creator of the universe (Excerpt from *Dare to Succeed by Breaking through Barriers* by Dr. Cassundra White-Elliott).

Where do our misconceptions come from? How is it that our self concepts get off kilter?

Low self esteem comes from negative patterns, such as those listed below:
1. Indulging in self-criticism.
   The enemy does an excellent job of criticizing you. Do not join his team and help in the criticism.
2. Neglecting personal needs by constantly seeking to please others.
   It is great to be considerate of others, but do not neglect yourself.
3. Trying to emulate someone else's style.
   God created each one of us to be a unique individual. Be proud of who you are.
4. Taking failures and the presence of problems too seriously.

Failure means you have not succeeded *yet.* Keep trying or alter the plan, but do not give up.

5. Living life by conditions and terms set by other people.

God is the one who set the standard for our lives. Living life as you choose within God's guidelines, without hurting others, is not a sin. What may be good for someone else may not be good for you.

6. Failing to recognize successes.

Focus on your accomplishments to demonstrate to yourself that you are capable of succeeding.

7. Speaking negatively.

Proverbs 18:21a says, *"Death and life are in the power of the tongue."* Speak life into your own situation by saying positive affirmations. Do not speak negative words because they breed death.

8. Focusing on past failures.

Learn from past mistakes, but let the past stay in the past.

(Excerpt from *Dare to Succeed by Breaking through Barriers* by Dr. Cassundra White-Elliott)

Knowing who you are has a lot to do with knowing your temperament, your personality, how you deal with things emotionally, physical attributes, strengths, weaknesses, etc. However, knowing yourself also encapsulates knowing which talent(s) God has embedded in you.

You were sent here to fulfill your purpose in this earthly realm. And, your talents assist you in fulfilling that purpose. But the key is- you must know what your purpose is. You must know how and why God has equipped you. Thus, you must know what your talents are.

Let us look at the prophet Jeremiah and the gift of prophecy he was given. In the book of Jeremiah, in the first chapter and the fifth verse, Jeremiah repeats the words that God said to him in an attempt to encourage him. Verse five reads: *"Before I formed thee in the belly I knew thee; and before thou camest forth out of the womb I sanctified thee, and I ordained thee a prophet unto the nations."* God told Jeremiah that He knew him before He formed him in his mother's womb. Then, God goes on to say that before He departed from His mother's womb, He sanctified him and ordained him.

Jeremiah had an assignment to deliver God's messages unto the people. However, the messages were not received. The people rejected the messages, and they rejected Jeremiah.

It is for this reason of rejection, amongst a host of others, people do not want to do what God has ordained them to do. They focus more on the discomforts of obedience than the rewards of obedience.

I Samuel 15:22 states, *"And Samuel said, Hath the LORD as great delight in burnt offerings and sacrifices, as in obeying the voice of the LORD? Behold, to obey is better than sacrifice, and to hearken than the fat of rams."*

Jeremiah was obedient to the call of God. But, yes he was afflicted along the way. Jeremiah 1:19 says, *"And they shall fight against thee; but they shall not prevail against thee; for I [am] with thee, saith the LORD, to deliver thee."*

Psalms 34:19 says, *"Many are the afflictions of the righteous: but the LORD delivereth him out of them all."*

We are encouraged to do the will of our Father. God did not promise us that our tasks would be easy. He did not promise us that we would not suffer along the way. But, He did promise us that He would protect us.

Jesus was afflicted for His teachings and His beliefs. Primarily though, He was afflicted simply for being just who he was. Our fate is no different. In Matthew 13:57, Jesus says, *"A prophet is not without honor except for in his own country and in his own house"* (biblehub.com/Jubilee Bible 2000).

Sometimes rejection will come, and people will not see the gifts that are within us. The key here is knowing who God says you are. Men may not always see your gift, but God knows what He deposited in you. In Acts 10:34, Peter tells us that God is *"no respecter of persons."*

Therefore, what God did for Jeremiah, He also did for you and for me. Like Jeremiah, before you were formed in your mother's womb and before I was formed in my mother's womb, God knew us and He specified a specific purpose for our lives. In order for us to carry out our individual purposes, God sanctified us and ordained us for a specific calling. What does it mean to be ordained and sanctified?

That means that in order for us to walk in our calling, God had to equip us with the ability to do exactly what He ordained us for and set us apart in the process.

If we survey the three synoptic gospels, we find that Jesus was always teaching and training His disciples on proper conduct as well as about the kingdom of heaven.

Jesus' primary method for teaching as demonstrated in these gospels was through the use of parables.

In the book of Matthew in the 25th chapter, beginning at verse 14, we find the parable of the talents. Here is our proof that God Himself is the giver of all gifts, which includes our talents. In this parable, we also see God's position on the abilities He gives to us. Verse fourteen reads, *"For the kingdom of heaven is as a man travelling into a far country, who called his own servants, and delivered unto them his goods."*

The first thing that we must note about Jesus' parables is that He did not simply tell His parables for the entertainment or amusement of the disciples. He wanted them to know about His father and how His father operated.

Let us translate the verse to see what is being said. The verse says- *the kingdom of heaven is as a man traveling into a far country*....the man who is traveling is representative of God, as God is the dispenser of 'goods.' And *the servants who were called* are the members of the body of Christ- us.

The very fact that He gave us gifts tells us that God has work for us to do, and He has assigned the work to our hands.

Now, as we go throughout the rest of the parable, I want you to place yourself into the place of one of the three servants that you will read about.

Verses 15-30 reads:

And unto one he gave five talents, to another two, and to another one; to every man according to his several ability; and straightway took his journey. Then he that had received the five talents went and traded with the

same, and made them other five talents. And likewise he
that had received two, he also gained other two. But he
that had received one went and digged in the earth, and
hid his lord's money. After a long time the lord of those
servants cometh, and reckoneth with them. And so he
that had received five talents came and brought other
five talents, saying, Lord, thou deliveredst unto me five
talents: behold, I have gained beside them five talents
more. His lord said unto him, Well done, thou good and
faithful servant: thou hast been faithful over a few
things, I will make thee ruler over many things: enter
thou into the joy of thy lord. He also that had received
two talents came and said, Lord, thou deliveredst unto
me two talents: behold, I have gained two other talents
beside them. His lord said unto him, Well done, good and
faithful servant; thou hast been faithful over a few
things, I will make thee ruler over many things: enter
thou into the joy of thy lord. Then he which had received
the one talent came and said, Lord, I knew thee that
thou art an hard man, reaping where thou hast not
sown, and gathering where thou hast not strawed: And I
was afraid, and went and hid thy talent in the earth: lo,
there thou hast that is thine. His lord answered and said
unto him, Thou wicked and slothful servant, thou
knewest that I reap where I sowed not, and gather
where I have not strawed: Thou oughtest therefore to
have put my money to the exchangers, and then at my
coming I should have received mine own with usury.
Take therefore the talent from him, and give it unto him
which hath ten talents. For unto every one that hath
shall be given, and he shall have abundance: but from
him that hath not shall be taken away even that which

he hath. And cast ye the unprofitable servant into outer darkness: there shall be weeping and gnashing of teeth.

It doesn't matter how many talents you have, what is important is that you activate your gift and use it to glorify God.

From the parable, we can see talents are not dispensed evenly. While one person may receive two talents, another person may only receive one, while yet another person may receive five. God, the Creator of all mankind, knows exactly who we are. He knows what He deposited in us, and He knows what we can handle because He knows how He made us.

As we commune with God, we get a better sense of our purpose. Each day we walk through this life, our destiny should become clearer and clearer.

However, there are times when we look at others' abilities and begin to question why we can't do what they can do. Obviously, God did not create all of us to be the same. We are uniquely designed individuals. Therefore, we will not all be given the same abilities. What God created me to do was not necessarily what He created you to do and vice versa.

Therefore, we should not consume ourselves with focusing on what others are doing and how they use their talents. Our responsibility to God is to use our talents to the best of our ability in an effort to fulfill His preordained plan for our lives.

Let's review the information that has been presented thus far:

1. God knew us before He drew us from our mother's womb.

2. God ordained and sanctified us by giving us talents to fulfill the calling on our lives.
3. We must recognize our gifts and use them.

Unfortunately, that is not enough. There is another important key. 1 Cor. 4:1-2 says, *"Let a man so account of us, as of the ministers of Christ, and stewards of the mysteries of God. Moreover it is required in stewards, that a man be found faithful."*

Not only must you recognize the fact that God has deposited talents in us to glorify Him and to edify His kingdom, He also wants us to be faithful over what He has placed into our hands. The more we use the talent, the more the talent will be perfected. For example, as a teacher, I am much better at explaining concepts and transferring knowledge today than I was twenty years ago. I am a much better writer today than I was ten or even five years ago. You will find the same to be true for you as you use your gifts continually month after month and year after year.

Let me close this chapter with a series of questions: When your race is over and you go to meet your maker, what will He say? Will He turn and say, "I never knew you"? Will He turn and say, "I gave you gifts but you only used them for material gain"? Will He turn and ask, "Why did you sit on the gifts that could have blessed so many people?" Or, will He smile upon you and say, "Well done, my good and faithful servant"?

In addition to God-given abilities, we have spiritual gifts bestowed upon us. Read through the following list of spiritual gifts and their respective definitions to see if you can identify any that you are blessed to have. If you do, use them according to God's plan for your life.

Definition of Spiritual Gifts Specifically Listed in the Bible:

ADMINISTRATION: 1 Cor. 12:28 - to steer the body toward the accomplishment of God-given goals and directives by planning, organizing, and supervising others

CELIBACY: 1 Cor. 7:7,8 - to voluntarily remain single without regret and with the ability to maintain controlled sexual impulses so as to serve the Lord without distraction

DISCERNMENT: 1 Cor. 12:10 - to clearly distinguish truth from error by judging whether the behavior or teaching is from God, Satan, human error, or human power

EVANGELISM: Eph. 4:11 - to be a messenger of the good news of the Gospel

EXHORTATION: Rom. 12:8 - to come along side of someone with words of encouragement, comfort, consolation, and counsel to help them be all God wants them to be

FAITH: 1 Cor. 12:8-10 - to be firmly persuaded of God's power and promises to accomplish His will and purpose and to display such a confidence in Him and His Word that circumstances and obstacles do not shake that conviction

GIVING: Rom. 12:8 - to share what material resources you have with liberality and cheerfulness without thought of return

HEALING: 1 Cor. 12:9,28,30 - to be used as a means through which God makes people whole either physically, emotionally, mentally, or spiritually

HELPS: 1 Cor. 12:28 - to render support or assistance to others in the body so as to free them up for ministry

HOSPITALITY: 1 Pet. 4:9,10 - to warmly welcome people, even strangers, into one's home or church as a means of serving those in need of food or lodging

KNOWLEDGE: 1 Cor. 12:8 - to seek to learn as much about the Bible as possible through the gathering of much information and the analyzing of that data

LEADERSHIP: Rom. 12:8 - to stand before the people in such a way as to attend to the direction of the body with such care and diligence so as to motivate others to get involved in the accomplishment of these goals

MARTYRDOM: 1 Cor. 13:3 - to give over one's life to suffer or to be put to death for the cause of Christ

MERCY: Rom. 12:8 - to be sensitive toward those who are suffering, whether physically, mentally, or emotionally, so as to feel genuine sympathy with their misery, speaking words of compassion but moreso caring for them with deeds of love to help alleviate their distress

MIRACLES: 1 Cor. 12:10,28 - to be enabled by God to perform mighty deeds which witnesses acknowledge to be of supernatural origin and means

MISSIONARY: Eph. 3:6-8 - to be able to minister in another culture

PASTOR: Eph. 4:11 - to be responsible for spiritually caring for, protecting, guiding, and feeding a group of believers entrusted to one's care

PROPHECY: Rom. 12:6; 1 Cor. 12:10; Eph. 4:11 - to speak forth the message of God to His people

SERVICE: Rom. 12:7 - to identify undone tasks in God's work, however menial, and use available resources to get the job done

TEACHING: Rom. 12:7; 1 Cor. 12:28; Eph. 4:11 - to instruct others in the Bible in a logical, systematic way so as to communicate pertinent information for true understanding and growth

TONGUES: 1 Cor. 12:10; 14:27-28 - to speak in a language not previously learned so unbelievers can hear God's message in their own language or the body be edified

INTERPRETATION OF TONGUES: 1 Cor. 12:10; 14:27,28 - to translate the message of someone who has spoken in tongues

VOLUNTARY POVERTY: 1 Cor. 13:3 - to purposely live an impoverished lifestyle to serve and aid others with your material resources

WISDOM: 1 Cor. 12:8 - to apply knowledge to life in such a way as to make spiritual truths quite relevant and practical in proper decision-making and daily life situations

4

Sisterly Love
(Build Your Sisters Up)

In Chapter Three, we examined who we are through a discussion of our God-given talents and our pre-determined and pre-ordained earthly purpose. Knowing who we are in Christ will assist us in being realistic about ourselves and our goals as well as how we see others, particularly other women.

The world we live in thrives off pitting one person against the other. Everything is about competition. The commercials on TV, the reality shows, and the Lifetime movies teach us we must be better than the next woman. We must look better, dress better, be smarter, better educated, have children who are more successful, etc. We have been programmed to compare ourselves with other women.

When a comparison is done, there are two likely results: either you will leave feeling better about yourself or worse. If you believe you fair better than your competitor, you will feel great. However, if you believe your competitor fairs better, you will feel pretty rotten. When we believe we have surpassed another woman, we can become lifted up in self-pride. When we believe we do not measure up, we can become consumed with bitterness toward others and ourselves.

Bitterness is the root cause of unforgiveness, which will eat away at us like a cancer.

Read the following scriptures below on bitterness to see what God says about this debilitating spirit (after the scriptures, read the story of Cain and Abel):

Ephesians 4:31-32 ESV
Let all bitterness and wrath and anger and clamor and slander be put away from you, along with all malice. Be kind to one another, tenderhearted, forgiving one another, as God in Christ forgave you.
Proverbs 15:1 ESV
A soft answer turns away wrath, but a harsh word stirs up anger.
Proverbs 20:22 ESV
Do not say, "I will repay evil"; wait for the Lord, and he will deliver you.
Ephesians 4:31 ESV
Let all bitterness and wrath and anger and clamor and slander be put away from you, along with all malice.
Matthew 6:14-15 ESV
For if you forgive others their trespasses, your heavenly Father will also forgive you, but if you do not forgive others their trespasses, neither will your Father forgive your trespasses.
James 1:19-20 ESV
Know this, my beloved brothers: let every person be quick to hear, slow to speak, slow to anger; for the anger of man does not produce the righteousness of God.

Hebrews 12:14-15 ESV

Strive for peace with everyone, and for the holiness without which no one will see the Lord. See to it that no one fails to obtain the grace of God; that no "root of bitterness" springs up and causes trouble, and by it many become defiled;

Hebrews 12:15 ESV

See to it that no one fails to obtain the grace of God; that no "root of bitterness" springs up and causes trouble, and by it many become defiled;

Proverbs 10:12 ESV

Hatred stirs up strife, but love covers all offenses.

Romans 12:17-21 ESV

Repay no one evil for evil, but give thought to do what is honorable in the sight of all. If possible, so far as it depends on you, live peaceably with all. Beloved, never avenge yourselves, but leave it to the wrath of God, for it is written, "Vengeance is mine, I will repay, says the Lord." To the contrary, "if your enemy is hungry, feed him; if he is thirsty, give him something to drink; for by so doing you will heap burning coals on his head." Do not be overcome by evil, but overcome evil with good.

James 1:26 ESV

If anyone thinks he is religious and does not bridle his tongue but deceives his heart, this person's religion is worthless.

Ephesians 4:26 ESV

Be angry and do not sin; do not let the sun go down on your anger,

Romans 12:2 ESV

Do not be conformed to this world, but be transformed by the renewal of your mind, that by testing you may discern what is the will of God, what is good and acceptable and perfect.

Mark 11:25 ESV

And whenever you stand praying, forgive, if you have anything against anyone, so that your Father also who is in heaven may forgive you your trespasses."

1 John 4:8 ESV

Anyone who does not love does not know God, because God is love.

Colossians 3:5-10 ESV

Put to death therefore what is earthly in you: sexual immorality, impurity, passion, evil desire, and covetousness, which is idolatry. On account of these the wrath of God is coming. In these you too once walked, when you were living in them. But now you must put them all away: anger, wrath, malice, slander, and obscene talk from your mouth. Do not lie to one another, seeing that you have put off the old self with its practices ...

Leviticus 19:18 ESV

You shall not take vengeance or bear a grudge against the sons of your own people, but you shall love your neighbor as yourself: I am the Lord.

James 4:1 ESV

What causes quarrels and what causes fights among you? Is it not this, that your passions are at war within you?

Romans 14:10-12 ESV

Why do you pass judgment on your brother? Or you, why do you despise your brother? For we will all stand before the judgment seat of God; for it is written, "As I live, says the Lord, every knee shall bow to me, and every tongue shall confess to God." So then each of us will give an account of himself to God.

Mark 12:31 ESV

The second is this: 'You shall love your neighbor as yourself.' There is no other commandment greater than these."

1 John 1:9 ESV

If we confess our sins, he is faithful and just to forgive us our sins and to cleanse us from all unrighteousness.

Colossians 3:8 ESV

But now you must put them all away: anger, wrath, malice, slander, and obscene talk from your mouth.

Matthew 15:18-19 ESV

But what comes out of the mouth proceeds from the heart, and this defiles a person. For out of the heart come evil thoughts, murder, adultery, sexual immorality, theft, false witness, slander.

1 Peter 5:8 ESV

Be sober-minded; be watchful. Your adversary the devil prowls around like a roaring lion, seeking someone to devour.

Proverbs 12:16 ESV

The vexation of a fool is known at once, but the prudent ignores an insult.

Romans 3:23 ESV

For all have sinned and fall short of the glory of God,

Luke 17:3-4 ESV

Pay attention to yourselves! If your brother sins, rebuke him, and if he repents, forgive him, and if he sins against you seven times in the day, and turns to you seven times, saying, 'I repent,' you must forgive him."

Mark 7:20-22 ESV

And he said, "What comes out of a person is what defiles him. For from within, out of the heart of man, come evil thoughts, sexual immorality, theft, murder, adultery, coveting, wickedness, deceit, sensuality, envy, slander, pride, foolishness.

Matthew 5:5-9 ESV

"Blessed are the meek, for they shall inherit the earth. "Blessed are those who hunger and thirst for righteousness, for they shall be satisfied. "Blessed are the merciful, for they shall receive mercy. "Blessed are the pure in heart, for they shall see God. "Blessed are the peacemakers, for they shall be called sons of God.

Colossians 3:7-8 ESV

In these you too once walked, when you were living in them. But now you must put them all away: anger, wrath, malice, slander, and obscene talk from your mouth.

James 2:12-13 ESV

So speak and so act as those who are to be judged under the law of liberty. For judgment is without mercy to one who has shown no mercy. Mercy triumphs over judgment.

Acts 8:23 ESV

For I see that you are in the gall of bitterness and in the bond of iniquity."

Ephesians 4:1-32 ESV

I therefore, a prisoner for the Lord, urge you to walk in a manner worthy of the calling to which you have been called, with all humility and gentleness, with patience, bearing with one another in love, eager to maintain the unity of the Spirit in the bond of peace. There is one body and one Spirit—just as you were called to the one hope that belongs to your call— one Lord, one faith, one baptism, ...

2 Timothy 2:15 ESV

Do your best to present yourself to God as one approved, a worker who has no need to be ashamed, rightly handling the word of truth.

Colossians 3:12-14 ESV

Put on then, as God's chosen ones, holy and beloved, compassionate hearts, kindness, humility, meekness, and patience, bearing with one another and, if one has a complaint against another, forgiving each other; as the Lord has forgiven you, so you also must forgive. And above all these put on love, which binds everything together in perfect harmony.

James 2:8 ESV

If you really fulfill the royal law according to the Scripture, "You shall love your neighbor as yourself," you are doing well.

Romans 2:21-24 ESV

You then who teach others, do you not teach yourself? While you preach against stealing, do you steal? You who say that one must not commit adultery, do you commit adultery? You who abhor idols, do you rob temples? You who boast in the law dishonor God by breaking the law. For, as it is written, "The name of God is blasphemed among the Gentiles because of you."

Hebrews 13:5 ESV

Keep your life free from love of money, and be content with what you have, for he has said, "I will never leave you nor forsake you."

Colossians 3:9 ESV

Do not lie to one another, seeing that you have put off the old self with its practices

Philippians 2:2-8 ESV

Complete my joy by being of the same mind, having the same love, being in full accord and of one mind. Do nothing from rivalry or conceit, but in humility count others more significant than yourselves. Let each of you look not only to his own interests, but also to the interests of others. Have this mind among yourselves, which is yours in Christ Jesus, who, though he was in the form of God, did not count equality with God a thing to be grasped, ...

Ephesians 4:32 ESV

Be kind to one another, tenderhearted, forgiving one another, as God in Christ forgave you.

Galatians 5:19-21 ESV

Now the works of the flesh are evident: sexual immorality, impurity, sensuality, idolatry, sorcery, enmity, strife, jealousy, fits of anger, rivalries, dissensions, divisions, envy, drunkenness, orgies, and things like these. I warn you, as I warned you before, that those who do such things will not inherit the kingdom of God.

Romans 13:8-10 ESV

Owe no one anything, except to love each other, for the one who loves another has fulfilled the law. For the commandments, "You shall not commit adultery, You shall not murder, You shall not steal, You shall not covet," and any other commandment, are summed up in this word: "You shall love your neighbor as yourself." Love does no wrong to a neighbor; therefore love is the fulfilling of the law.

Romans 2:1-4 ESV

Therefore you have no excuse, O man, every one of you who judges. For in passing judgment on another you condemn yourself, because you, the judge, practice the very same things. We know that the judgment of God rightly falls on those who practice such things. Do you suppose, O man— you who judge those who practice such things and yet do them yourself—that you will escape the judgment of God? Or do you presume on the riches of his kindness and forbearance and patience, not knowing that God's kindness is meant to lead you to repentance?

Luke 6:32-42 ESV

If you love those who love you, what benefit is that to you? For even sinners love those who love them. And if you do good to those who do good to you, what benefit is that to you? For even sinners do the same. And if you lend to those from whom you expect to receive, what credit is that to you? Even sinners lend to sinners, to get back the same amount. But love your enemies, and do good, and lend, expecting nothing in return, and your reward will be great, and you will be sons of the Most High, for he is kind to the ungrateful and the evil. Be merciful, even as your Father is merciful. ...

James 3:1-18 ESV

Not many of you should become teachers, my brothers, for you know that we who teach will be judged with greater strictness. For we all stumble in many ways. And if anyone does not stumble in what he says, he is a perfect man, able also to bridle his whole body. If we put bits into the mouths of horses so that they obey us, we guide their whole bodies as well. Look at the ships also: though they are so large and are driven by strong winds, they are guided by a very small rudder wherever the will of the pilot directs. So also the tongue is a small member, yet it boasts of great things. How great a forest is set ablaze by such a small fire! ...

Hebrews 13:15-16 ESV

Through him then let us continually offer up a sacrifice of praise to God, that is, the fruit of lips that acknowledge his name. Do not neglect to do good and to share what you have, for such sacrifices are pleasing to God.

Romans 12:6-8 ESV

Having gifts that differ according to the grace given to us, let us use them: if prophecy, in proportion to our faith; if service, in our serving; the one who teaches, in his teaching; the one who exhorts, in his exhortation; the one who contributes, in generosity; the one who leads, with zeal; the one who does acts of mercy, with cheerfulness.

Acts 20:35 ESV

In all things I have shown you that by working hard in this way we must help the weak and remember the words of the Lord Jesus, how he himself said, 'It is more blessed to give than to receive.'

Acts 2:38 ESV

And Peter said to them, "Repent and be baptized every one of you in the name of Jesus Christ for the forgiveness of your sins, and you will receive the gift of the Holy Spirit.

John 13:34-35 ESV

A new commandment I give to you, that you love one another: just as I have loved you, you also are to love one another. By this all people will know that you are my disciples, if you have love for one another.

John 8:1-8 ESV

But Jesus went to the Mount of Olives. Early in the morning he came again to the temple. All the people came to him, and he sat down and taught them. The scribes and the Pharisees brought a woman who had been caught in adultery, and placing her in the midst they said to him, "Teacher, this woman has been caught in the act of adultery. Now in the Law Moses commanded us to stone such women. So what do you say?" ...

Luke 6:31 ESV

And as you wish that others would do to you, do so to them.

Matthew 18:21-22 ESV

Then Peter came up and said to him, "Lord, how often will my brother sin against me, and I forgive him? As many as seven times?" Jesus said to him, "I do not say to you seven times, but seventy times seven.

Matthew 18:15 ESV

"If your brother sins against you, go and tell him his fault, between you and him alone. If he listens to you, you have gained your brother.

Matthew 7:21-23 ESV

"Not everyone who says to me, 'Lord, Lord,' will enter the kingdom of heaven, but the one who does the will of my Father who is in heaven. On that day many will say to me, 'Lord, Lord, did we not prophesy in your name, and cast out demons in your name, and do many mighty works in your name?' And then will I declare to them, 'I never knew you; depart from me, you workers of lawlessness.'

Matthew 6:1-2 ESV

"Beware of practicing your righteousness before other people in order to be seen by them, for then you will have no reward from your Father who is in heaven. "Thus, when you give to the needy, sound no trumpet before you, as the hypocrites do in the synagogues and in the streets, that they may be praised by others. Truly, I say to you, they have received their reward.

Matthew 5:43-48 ESV

"You have heard that it was said, 'You shall love your neighbor and hate your enemy.' But I say to you, Love your enemies and pray for those who persecute you, so that you may be sons of your Father who is in heaven. For he makes his sun rise on the evil and on the good, and sends rain on the just and on the unjust. For if you love those who love you, what reward do you have? Do not even the tax collectors do the same? And if you greet only your brothers, what more are you doing than others? Do not even the Gentiles do the same? ...

Matthew 5:43-45 ESV

"You have heard that it was said, 'You shall love your neighbor and hate your enemy.' But I say to you, Love your enemies and pray for those who persecute you, so that you may be sons of your Father who is in heaven. For he makes his sun rise on the evil and on the good, and sends rain on the just and on the unjust.

Matthew 5:42 ESV

Give to the one who begs from you, and do not refuse the one who would borrow from you.

Ecclesiastes 12:13-14 ESV

The end of the matter; all has been heard. Fear God and keep his commandments, for this is the whole duty of man. For God will bring every deed into judgment, with every secret thing, whether good or evil.

Ecclesiastes 7:9 ESV

Be not quick in your spirit to become angry, for anger lodges in the bosom of fools.

Proverbs 12:22 ESV

Lying lips are an abomination to the Lord, but those who act faithfully are his delight.

Psalm 37:8-9 ESV

Refrain from anger, and forsake wrath! Fret not yourself; it tends only to evil. For the evildoers shall be cut off, but those who wait for the Lord shall inherit the land.

1 John 2:9-11 ESV

Whoever says he is in the light and hates his brother is still in darkness. Whoever loves his brother abides in the light, and in him there is no cause for stumbling. But whoever hates his brother is in the darkness and walks in the darkness, and does not know where he is going, because the darkness has blinded his eyes.

James 4:11-12 ESV

Do not speak evil against one another, brothers. The one who speaks against a brother or judges his brother, speaks evil against the law and judges the law. But if you judge the law, you are not a doer of the law but a judge. There is only one lawgiver and judge, he who is able to save and to destroy. But who are you to judge your neighbor?

James 3:11 ESV

Does a spring pour forth from the same opening both fresh and salt water?

James 2:1 ESV

My brothers, show no partiality as you hold the faith in our Lord Jesus Christ, the Lord of glory.

James 1:22-27 ESV

But be doers of the word, and not hearers only, deceiving yourselves. For if anyone is a hearer of the word and not a doer, he is like a man who looks intently at his natural face in a mirror. For he looks at himself and goes away and at once forgets what he was like. But the one who looks into the perfect law, the law of liberty, and perseveres, being no hearer who forgets but a doer who acts, he will be blessed in his doing. If anyone thinks he is religious and does not bridle his tongue but deceives his heart, this person's religion is worthless. ...

Hebrews 13:1-3 ESV

Let brotherly love continue. Do not neglect to show hospitality to strangers, for thereby some have entertained angels unawares. Remember those who are in prison, as though in prison with them, and those who are mistreated, since you also are in the body.

Hebrews 13:1 ESV

Let brotherly love continue.

Colossians 3:19 ESV

Husbands, love your wives, and do not be harsh with them.

Colossians 3:5 ESV

Put to death therefore what is earthly in you: sexual immorality, impurity, passion, evil desire, and covetousness, which is idolatry.

Philippians 4:8-9 ESV

Finally, brothers, whatever is true, whatever is honorable, whatever is just, whatever is pure, whatever is lovely, whatever is commendable, if there is any excellence, if there is anything worthy of praise, think about these things. What you have learned and received and heard and seen in me— practice these things, and the God of peace will be with you.

Ephesians 5:1-7 ESV

Therefore be imitators of God, as beloved children. And walk in love, as Christ loved us and gave himself up for us, a fragrant offering and sacrifice to God. But sexual immorality and all impurity or covetousness must not even be named among you, as is proper among saints. Let there be no filthiness nor foolish talk nor crude joking, which are out of place, but instead let there be thanksgiving. For you may be sure of this, that everyone who is sexually immoral or impure, or who is covetous (that is, an idolater), has no inheritance in the kingdom of Christ and God. ...

Ephesians 4:25 ESV

Therefore, having put away falsehood, let each one of you speak the truth with his neighbor, for we are members one of another.

Ephesians 4:1-6 ESV

I therefore, a prisoner for the Lord, urge you to walk in a manner worthy of the calling to which you have been called, with all humility and gentleness, with patience, bearing with one another in love, eager to maintain the unity of the Spirit in the bond of peace. There is one body and one Spirit—just as you were called to the one hope that belongs to your call— one Lord, one faith, one baptism, ...

Galatians 6:7-8 ESV

Do not be deceived: God is not mocked, for whatever one sows, that will he also reap. For the one who sows to his own flesh will from the flesh reap corruption, but the one who sows to the Spirit will from the Spirit reap eternal life.

Galatians 6:1-3 ESV

Brothers, if anyone is caught in any transgression, you who are spiritual should restore him in a spirit of gentleness. Keep watch on yourself, lest you too be tempted. Bear one another's burdens, and so fulfill the law of Christ. For if anyone thinks he is something, when he is nothing, he deceives himself.

Galatians 5:16-26 ESV

But I say, walk by the Spirit, and you will not gratify the desires of the flesh. For the desires of the flesh are against the Spirit, and the desires of the Spirit are against the flesh, for these are opposed to each other, to keep you from doing the things you want to do. But if you are led by the Spirit, you are not under the law. Now the works of the flesh are evident: sexual immorality, impurity, sensuality, idolatry, sorcery, enmity, strife, jealousy, fits of anger, rivalries, dissensions, divisions, ...

2 Corinthians 5:1 ESV

For we know that if the tent that is our earthly home is destroyed, we have a building from God, a house not made with hands, eternal in the heavens.

Romans 15:1-2 ESV

We who are strong have an obligation to bear with the failings of the weak, and not to please ourselves. Let each of us please his neighbor for his good, to build him up.

Romans 14:1 ESV

As for the one who is weak in faith, welcome him, but not to quarrel over opinions.

Romans 13:1 ESV

Let every person be subject to the governing authorities. For there is no authority except from God, and those that exist have been instituted by God.

Romans 12:1 ESV

I appeal to you therefore, brothers, by the mercies of God, to present your bodies as a living sacrifice, holy and acceptable to God, which is your spiritual worship.

Romans 8:28 ESV

And we know that for those who love God all things work together for good, for those who are called according to his purpose.

John 3:17 ESV

For God did not send his Son into the world to condemn the world, but in order that the world might be saved through him.

Luke 6:37 ESV

"Judge not, and you will not be judged; condemn not, and you will not be condemned; forgive, and you will be forgiven;

Luke 3:12-14 ESV

Tax collectors also came to be baptized and said to him, "Teacher, what shall we do?" And he said to them, "Collect no more than you are authorized to do." Soldiers also asked him, "And we, what shall we do?" And he said to them, "Do not extort money from anyone by threats or by false accusation, and be content with your wages."

Matthew 18:21-35 ESV

Then Peter came up and said to him, "Lord, how often will my brother sin against me, and I forgive him? As many as seven times?" Jesus said to him, "I do not say to you seven times, but seventy times seven. "Therefore the kingdom of heaven may be compared to a king who wished to settle accounts with his servants. When he began to settle, one was brought to him who owed him ten thousand talents. And since he could not pay, his master ordered him to be sold, with his wife and children and all that he had, and payment to be made. ...

Matthew 15:7-9 ESV

You hypocrites! Well did Isaiah prophesy of you, when he said: "'This people honors me with their lips, but their heart is far from me; in vain do they worship me, teaching as doctrines the commandments of men.'"

Matthew 7:12 ESV

"So whatever you wish that others would do to you, do also to them, for this is the Law and the Prophets.

Matthew 7:1-5 ESV

"Judge not, that you be not judged. For with the judgment you pronounce you will be judged, and with the measure you use it will be measured to you. Why do you see the speck that is in your brother's eye, but do not notice the log that is in your own eye? Or how can you say to your brother, 'Let me take the speck out of your eye,' when there is the log in your own eye? You hypocrite, first take the log out of your own eye, and then you will see clearly to take the speck out of your brother's eye.

Matthew 6:31-34 ESV

Therefore do not be anxious, saying, 'What shall we eat?' or 'What shall we drink?' or 'What shall we wear?' For the Gentiles seek after all these things, and your heavenly Father knows that you need them all. But seek first the kingdom of God and his righteousness, and all these things will be added to you. "Therefore do not be anxious about tomorrow, for tomorrow will be anxious for itself. Sufficient for the day is its own trouble.

Matthew 6:24 ESV

"No one can serve two masters, for either he will hate the one and love the other, or he will be devoted to the one and despise the other. You cannot serve God and money.

Matthew 6:1-7 ESV

"Beware of practicing your righteousness before other people in order to be seen by them, for then you will have no reward from your Father who is in heaven. "Thus, when you give to the needy, sound no trumpet before you, as the hypocrites do in the synagogues and in the streets, that they may be praised by others. Truly, I say to you, they have received their reward. But when you give to the needy, do not let your left hand know what your right hand is doing, so that your giving may be in secret. And your Father who sees in secret will reward you. "And when you pray, you must not be like the hypocrites. For they love to stand and pray in the synagogues and at the street corners, that they may be seen by others. Truly, I say to you, they have received their reward. ...

Matthew 5:38-40 ESV

"You have heard that it was said, 'An eye for an eye and a tooth for a tooth.' But I say to you, Do not resist the one who is evil. But if anyone slaps you on the right cheek, turn to him the other also. And if anyone would sue you and take your tunic, let him have your cloak as well.

Proverbs 24:29 ESV

Do not say, "I will do to him as he has done to me; I will pay the man back for what he has done."

Proverbs 19:11 ESV

Good sense makes one slow to anger, and it is his glory to overlook an offense.

Proverbs 19:1 ESV

Better is a poor person who walks in his integrity than one who is crooked in speech and is a fool.

Job 10:1 ESV

"I loathe my life; I will give free utterance to my complaint; I will speak in the bitterness of my soul.

Deuteronomy 15:7-11 ESV

"If among you, one of your brothers should become poor, in any of your towns within your land that the Lord your God is giving you, you shall not harden your heart or shut your hand against your poor brother, but you shall open your hand to him and lend him sufficient for his need, whatever it may be. Take care lest there be an unworthy thought in your heart and you say, 'The seventh year, the year of release is near,' and your eye look grudgingly on your poor brother, and you give him nothing, and he cry to the Lord against you, and you be guilty of sin. You shall give to him freely, and your heart shall not be grudging when you give to him, because for this the Lord your God will bless you in all your work and in all that you undertake. For there will never cease to be poor in the land. Therefore I command you, 'You shall open wide your hand to your brother, to the needy and to the poor, in your land.'

1 John 3:1-2 ESV

See what kind of love the Father has given to us, that we should be called children of God; and so we are. The reason why the world does not know us is that it did not know him. Beloved, we are God's children now, and what we will be has not yet appeared; but we know that when he appears we shall be like him, because we shall see him as he is.

James 2:14-24 ESV

What good is it, my brothers, if someone says he has faith but does not have works? Can that faith save him? If a brother or sister is poorly clothed and lacking in daily food, and one of you says to them, "Go in peace, be warmed and filled," without giving them the things needed for the body, what good is that? So also faith by itself, if it does not have works, is dead. But someone will say, "You have faith and I have works." Show me your faith apart from your works, and I will show you my faith by my works. ...

Philippians 2:2 ESV

Complete my joy by being of the same mind, having the same love, being in full accord and of one mind.

2 Corinthians 4:17 ESV

For this light momentary affliction is preparing for us an eternal weight of glory beyond all comparison,

1 Corinthians 10:13 ESV

No temptation has overtaken you that is not common to man. God is faithful, and he will not let you be tempted beyond your ability, but with the temptation he will also provide the way of escape, that you may be able to endure it.

1 Corinthians 6:1-6 ESV

When one of you has a grievance against another, does he dare go to law before the unrighteous instead of the saints? Or do you not know that the saints will judge the world? And if the world is to be judged by you, are you incompetent to try trivial cases? Do you not know that we are to judge angels? How much more, then, matters pertaining to this life! So if you have such cases, why do you lay them before those who have no standing in the church? I say this to your shame. Can it be that there is no one among you wise enough to settle a dispute between the brothers, ...

Romans 8:18 ESV

For I consider that the sufferings of this present time are not worth comparing with the glory that is to be revealed to us.

John 16:33 ESV

I have said these things to you, that in me you may have peace. In the world you will have tribulation. But take heart; I have overcome the world."

Luke 7:36-50 ESV

One of the Pharisees asked him to eat with him, and he went into the Pharisee's house and took his place at the table. And behold, a woman of the city, who was a sinner, when she learned that he was reclining at table in the Pharisee's house, brought an alabaster flask of ointment, and standing behind him at his feet, weeping, she began to wet his feet with her tears and wiped them with the hair of her head and kissed his feet and anointed them with the ointment. Now when the Pharisee who had invited him saw this, he said to himself, "If this man were a prophet, he would have known who and what sort of woman this is who is touching him, for she is a sinner." And Jesus answering said to him, "Simon, I have something to say to you." And he answered, "Say it, Teacher." ...

Luke 1:1-80 ESV

Inasmuch as many have undertaken to compile a narrative of the things that have been accomplished among us, just as those who from the beginning were eyewitnesses and ministers of the word have delivered them to us, it seemed good to me also, having followed all things closely for some time past, to write an orderly account for you, most excellent Theophilus, that you may have certainty concerning the things you have been taught. In the days of Herod, king of Judea, there was a priest named Zechariah, of the division of Abijah. And he had a wife from the daughters of Aaron, and her name was Elizabeth. ...

Mark 12:28-31 ESV

And one of the scribes came up and heard them disputing with one another, and seeing that he answered them well, asked him, "Which commandment is the most important of all?" Jesus answered, "The most important is, 'Hear, O Israel: The Lord our God, the Lord is one. And you shall love the Lord your God with all your heart and with all your soul and with all your mind and with all your strength.' The second is this: 'You shall love your neighbor as yourself.' There is no other commandment greater than these."

Mark 12:28-30 ESV

And one of the scribes came up and heard them disputing with one another, and seeing that he answered them well, asked him, "Which commandment is the most important of all?" Jesus answered, "The most important is, 'Hear, O Israel: The Lord our God, the Lord is one. And you shall love the Lord your God with all your heart and with all your soul and with all your mind and with all your strength.'

Mark 10:11-12 ESV

And he said to them, "Whoever divorces his wife and marries another commits adultery against her, and if she divorces her husband and marries another, she commits adultery."

Mark 9:35 ESV

And he sat down and called the twelve. And he said to them, "If anyone would be first, he must be last of all and servant of all."

Mark 9:1 ESV

And he said to them, "Truly, I say to you, there are some standing here who will not taste death until they see the kingdom of God after it has come with power."

Matthew 25:31-46 ESV

"When the Son of Man comes in his glory, and all the angels with him, then he will sit on his glorious throne. Before him

will be gathered all the nations, and he will separate people one from another as a shepherd separates the sheep from the goats. And he will place the sheep on his right, but the goats on the left. Then the King will say to those on his right, 'Come, you who are blessed by my Father, inherit the kingdom prepared for you from the foundation of the world. For I was hungry and you gave me food, I was thirsty and you gave me drink, I was a stranger and you welcomed me.

Matthew 23:1-33 ESV

Then Jesus said to the crowds and to his disciples, "The scribes and the Pharisees sit on Moses' seat, so practice and observe whatever they tell you—but not what they do. For they preach, but do not practice. They tie up heavy burdens, hard to bear, and lay them on people's shoulders, but they themselves are not willing to move them with their finger. They do all their deeds to be seen by others. For they make their phylacteries broad and their fringes long, ...

Matthew 22:34-40 ESV

But when the Pharisees heard that he had silenced the Sadducees, they gathered together. And one of them, a lawyer, asked him a question to test him. "Teacher, which is the great commandment in the Law?" And he said to him, "You shall love the Lord your God with all your heart and with all your soul and with all your mind. This is the great and first commandment. ...

Matthew 20:25-28 ESV

But Jesus called them to him and said, "You know that the rulers of the Gentiles lord it over them, and their great ones exercise authority over them. It shall not be so among you. But whoever would be great among you must be your servant, and whoever would be first among you must be your slave, even as the Son of Man came not to be served but to serve, and to give his life as a ransom for many."

Matthew 20:20-28 ESV

Then the mother of the sons of Zebedee came up to him with her sons, and kneeling before him she asked him for something. And he said to her, "What do you want?" She said to him, "Say that these two sons of mine are to sit, one at your right hand and one at your left, in your kingdom." Jesus answered, "You do not know what you are asking. Are you able to drink the cup that I am to drink?" They said to him, "We are able." He said to them, "You will drink my cup, but to sit at my right hand and at my left is not mine to grant, but it is for those for whom it has been prepared by my Father." And when the ten heard it, they were indignant at the two brothers. ...

Matthew 18:10 ESV

See that you do not despise one of these little ones. For I tell you that in heaven their angels always see the face of my Father who is in heaven.

Matthew 16:26 ESV

For what will it profit a man if he gains the whole world and forfeits his soul? Or what shall a man give in return for his soul?

Matthew 9:10-13 ESV

And as Jesus reclined at table in the house, behold, many tax collectors and sinners came and were reclining with Jesus and his disciples. And when the Pharisees saw this, they said to his disciples, "Why does your teacher eat with tax collectors and sinners?" But when he heard it, he said, "Those who are well have no need of a physician, but those who are sick. Go and learn what this means, 'I desire mercy, and not sacrifice.' For I came not to call the righteous, but sinners."

Matthew 7:15-20 ESV

Beware of false prophets, who come to you in sheep's clothing but inwardly are ravenous wolves. You will recognize them by their fruits. Are grapes gathered from thornbushes, or figs from thistles? So, every healthy tree bears good fruit, but the diseased tree bears bad fruit. A healthy tree cannot bear bad fruit, nor can a diseased tree bear good fruit. Every tree that does not bear good fruit is cut down and thrown into the fire. ...

Matthew 5:27-28 ESV

You have heard that it was said, 'You shall not commit adultery.' But I say to you that everyone who looks at a woman with lustful intent has already committed adultery with her in his heart.

Matthew 5:21-26 ESV

You have heard that it was said to those of old, 'You shall not murder; and whoever murders will be liable to judgment.' But I say to you that everyone who is angry with his brother will be liable to judgment; whoever insults his brother will be liable to the council; and whoever says, 'You fool!' will be liable to the hell of fire. So if you are offering your gift at the altar and there remember that your brother has something against you, leave your gift there before the altar and go. First be reconciled to your brother, and then come and offer your gift. Come to terms quickly with your accuser while you are going with him to court, lest your accuser hand you over to the judge, and the judge to the guard, and you be put in prison. ...

Matthew 5:7 ESV

Blessed are the merciful, for they shall receive mercy.

Zechariah 7:9 ESV

"Thus says the Lord of hosts, Render true judgments, show kindness and mercy to one another,

Isaiah 38:17 ESV

Behold, it was for my welfare that I had great bitterness; but in love you have delivered my life from the pit of destruction, for you have cast all my sins behind your back.

Proverbs 28:13 ESV

Whoever conceals his transgressions will not prosper, but he who confesses and forsakes them will obtain mercy.

Psalm 32:1-7 ESV

A Maskil of David. Blessed is the one whose transgression is forgiven, whose sin is covered. Blessed is the man against whom the Lord counts no iniquity, and in whose spirit there is no deceit. For when I kept silent, my bones wasted away through my groaning all day long. For day and night your hand was heavy upon me; my strength was dried up as by the heat of summer. Selah I acknowledged my sin to you, and I did not cover my iniquity; I said, "I will confess my transgressions to the Lord," and you forgave the iniquity of my sin. Selah ...

Psalm 31:10 ESV

For my life is spent with sorrow, and my years with sighing; my strength fails because of my iniquity, and my bones waste away.

1 Samuel 1:10 ESV

She was deeply distressed and prayed to the Lord and wept bitterly.

Leviticus 25:35-38 ESV

"If your brother becomes poor and cannot maintain himself with you, you shall support him as though he were a stranger and a sojourner, and he shall live with you. Take no interest from him or profit, but fear your God, that your brother may live beside you. You shall not lend him your money at interest, nor give him your food for profit. I am the

Lord your God, who brought you out of the land of Egypt to give you the land of Canaan, and to be your God.

Genesis 37:18-28 ESV

They saw him from afar, and before he came near to them they conspired against him to kill him. They said to one another, "Here comes this dreamer. Come now, let us kill him and throw him into one of the pits. Then we will say that a fierce animal has devoured him, and we will see what will become of his dreams." But when Reuben heard it, he rescued him out of their hands, saying, "Let us not take his life." And Reuben said to them, "Shed no blood; throw him into this pit here in the wilderness, but do not lay a hand on him"—that he might rescue him out of their hand to restore him to his father. ...

Luke 21:1-4 ESV

Jesus looked up and saw the rich putting their gifts into the offering box, and he saw a poor widow put in two small copper coins. And he said, "Truly, I tell you, this poor widow has put in more than all of them. For they all contributed out of their abundance, but she out of her poverty put in all she had to live on."

Luke 16:13 ESV

No servant can serve two masters, for either he will hate the one and love the other, or he will be devoted to the one and despise the other. You cannot serve God and money."

Luke 16:10-12 ESV

"One who is faithful in a very little is also faithful in much, and one who is dishonest in a very little is also dishonest in much. If then you have not been faithful in the unrighteous wealth, who will entrust to you the true riches? And if you have not been faithful in that which is another's, who will give you that which is your own?

Luke 12:33 ESV

Sell your possessions, and give to the needy. Provide yourselves with moneybags that do not grow old, with a treasure in the heavens that does not fail, where no thief approaches and no moth destroys.

Luke 10:25-28 ESV

And behold, a lawyer stood up to put him to the test, saying, "Teacher, what shall I do to inherit eternal life?" He said to him, "What is written in the Law? How do you read it?" And he answered, "You shall love the Lord your God with all your heart and with all your soul and with all your strength and with all your mind, and your neighbor as yourself." And he said to him, "You have answered correctly; do this, and you will live."

Luke 6:38 ESV

Give, and it will be given to you. Good measure, pressed down, shaken together, running over, will be put into your lap. For with the measure you use it will be measured back to you."

Isaiah 58:10-11 ESV

If you pour yourself out for the hungry and satisfy the desire of the afflicted, then shall your light rise in the darkness and your gloom be as the noonday. And the Lord will guide you continually and satisfy your desire in scorched places and make your bones strong; and you shall be like a watered garden, like a spring of water, whose waters do not fail.

Acts 14:11-15 ESV

And when the crowds saw what Paul had done, they lifted up their voices, saying in Lycaonian, "The gods have come down to us in the likeness of men!" Barnabas they called Zeus, and Paul, Hermes, because he was the chief speaker. And the priest of Zeus, whose temple was at the entrance to the city, brought oxen and garlands to the gates and wanted to offer sacrifice with the crowds. But when the apostles Barnabas and Paul heard of it, they tore their garments and rushed out into the crowd, crying out, "Men, why are you doing these things? We also are men, of like nature with you, and we bring you good news, that you should turn from these vain things to a living God, who made the heaven and the earth and the sea and all that is in them.

To understand how far bitterness can drive a person, let's review the story of a relationship between brothers-Cain and Abel- in Genesis Chapter 4:

Adam made love to his wife Eve, and she became pregnant and gave birth to Cain. She said, "With the help of the LORD I have brought forth a man." ² Later she gave birth to his brother Abel. Now Abel kept flocks, and Cain worked the soil. ³ In the course of time Cain brought some of the fruits of the soil as an offering to the LORD. ⁴ And Abel also brought an offering—fat portions from some of the firstborn of his flock. The LORD looked with favor on Abel and his offering, ⁵ but on Cain and his offering he did not look with favor. So Cain was very angry, and his face was downcast. ⁶ Then the LORD said to Cain, "Why are you angry? Why is your face downcast? ⁷ If you do what is right, will you not be accepted? But if you do not do what is right, sin is crouching at your door; it desires to have you, but you must rule over it." ⁸ Now Cain said to his brother Abel, "Let's go out to the field." While they were in the field, Cain attacked his brother Abel and killed him. ⁹ Then the LORD said to Cain, "Where is your brother Abel?" "I don't know," he replied. "Am I my brother's keeper?" ¹⁰ The LORD said, "What have you done? Listen! Your brother's *blood cries out to me from the ground. ¹¹ Now you are under a curse and driven from the ground, which opened its mouth to receive your brother's blood from your hand. ¹² When you work the ground, it will no longer yield its crops for you. You will be a restless wanderer on the earth." ¹³ Cain said to the LORD, "My punishment is more than I can bear. ¹⁴ Today you are driving me from the land, and I will be hidden from your presence; I will be a restless wanderer on the earth, and whoever finds me will kill me." ¹⁵ But the LORD said to him, "Not so; anyone who kills Cain will suffer vengeance seven times over." Then the LORD put a mark on Cain so that no one who found him would kill him. ¹⁶ So Cain went out from the LORD's presence and lived in the land of Nod, east of Eden.* (biblegateway.com/NIV)

Both Cain and Abel were obedient in offering a sacrifice unto the Lord. However, something went very wrong. When God surveyed what the two brothers brought before Him, He favored what Abel had brought, but looked unfavorably upon what Cain had brought. God's favor upon Abel sparked envy within Cain. The spirit of envy led to Cain experiencing uncontrollable anger. Instead of Cain admitting his shortcomings in his offering unto the Lord, he turned his frustrations and disappointments toward his brother. Eventually, the spirit of anger and its detrimental hold led Cain to committing the first recorded murder against his own flesh and blood-his younger brother Abel.

Realistically, the story of Cain and Abel is a little hard to fathom. We all know siblings argue and even have physical altercations. However, most of us do not know anyone who has resorted to murder. Murder is not the point here. The point for sharing the story of Cain and Abel is to show how we as humans tend to behave irrationally rather than taking responsibility in life.

Like Cain, many people blame others for their failures or shortcomings. In the case of the brothers, Cain may have felt if his brother wasn't doing such a fantastic job, he would not look so bad. Many women today think this same way. They always survey who their competition is and try to outdo the competition rather than simply focusing on doing their best.

Today, women will look for flaws in another woman's character, make up, dress, attitude, etc. in order to appear 'better' than she is.

Why is it that we must be better than one another? The world believes in the pyramid hierarchical structure. However, this not how God designed life to be. Think about God Himself when He said, "Let us make man in our image." He said 'our' image, not 'my image.' In order to make someone in the image of multiple identities (Father, Son and Holy Spirit), the multiple identities must share the same characteristics. We do not see the Father, Son, and Holy Spirit fighting for positions and titles. Each has His role and the support of the other. Jesus said, *"I come to do the will of my father."* Jesus is not intimidated by God, the Father, nor is He trying to take over the position of the Father.

The harmonious interaction of the Godhead is our example of how we are to co-exist with our sisters. We should not focus our attention on how we can beat each other down. Rather, we should be concerned with how we can lift each other up and assist one another with our goals. Our sister's back is not an excellent stepping-stone to our success or an excellent body part to stab. It is a point of contact to rub and encourage.

5

Women in Ministry
(A Vessel of Honor)

A woman involved in ministry has not always had the easiest time, especially while serving as an evangelist, minister, or teacher. We will not even open a discussion on a woman serving as a pastor or an apostle and the treatment she receives. It has been the perspective of many that women should not lead in church or speak from the pulpit.

However, over time, this narrow-minded, provincial perspective has begun to evolve. Has the word of God changed? No, it has not. Maybe the heart of man has changed, or the biblical interpretations regarding women in ministry have changed. If you share the perspective that it is not God's design for women to work in ministry, continue reading this chapter and see if your perspective changes.

All in all, whether women are readily accepted in ministry or whether they experience rejection, if they serve in ministry, they must ascertain what type of vessel they are and if their service is pleasing to God. All servants of God should strive to be vessels of honor.

Read II Timothy 2:20-26:

But in a great house there are not only vessels of gold and of silver, but also of wood and of earth; and some to honour, and some to dishonour. If a man therefore purge himself from these, he shall be a vessel unto honour, sanctified, and meet for the master's use, and prepared unto every good work. Flee also youthful lusts: but follow righteousness, faith, charity, peace, with them that call on the Lord out of a pure heart. But foolish and unlearned questions avoid, knowing that they do gender strifes. And the servant of the Lord must not strive; but be gentle unto all men, apt to teach, patient, In meekness instructing those that oppose themselves; if God peradventure will give them repentance to the acknowledging of the truth; And that they may recover themselves out of the snare of the devil, who are taken captive by him at his will.

In the above verses, Apostle Paul tells us in a well-furnished kitchen, there are not only crystal goblets and silver platters, but also waste cans and compost buckets. Some containers are used to serve fine meals, while others are used to take out the garbage. We should strive to become the kind of container God can use to present any and every kind of gift to lost souls and believers alike.

Apostle Paul teaches us three things in this passage of Scripture.

Both vessels are in the house.

This is not a message for non-Christians. This lesson concerning the use of our vessel is a lesson for Christians. When he makes the statement that there are vessels of honor and vessels of dishonor in the house he is not comparing Christians and non-Christians. He is dealing with Christians alone.

There are two types of Christians.

There are Christians who have become vessels of honor and some who have become vessels of dishonor. What makes us one or the other? What determines if we are a vessel of honor or dishonor? According to Apostle Paul, the difference is determined by how we choose to use or handle our vessel.

When God looks at us and examines how we handle our vessel, some of us look like gold/silver while some of us look like Styrofoam.

How we use our bodies determines the type of vessels we are.

Apostle Paul clearly states that how we choose to use our body determines how God will use us. It is when we choose to become a vessel of honor that we are fit for every good work. But you can read what is not stated and realize that if we choose not to handle our vessel as one of honor, we will not be fit for the work of the Lord.

As you prepare yourself for ministry or continue to serve in ministry, ask yourself the following questions. What type of vessel are you? Are you a vessel that brings glory and honor to God? Are you a vessel that dishonors God by the very acts that you commit with your body that is meant to be a holy dwelling place for God? To help you view your current position in ministry and how you are presenting yourself before God, read the following accounts of three women who were used in ministry in different capacities:

Deborah

Deborah, a prophetess, the wife of Lapidoth, judged Israel at that time. And she dwelt under the palm tree of Deborah between Ramah and Bethel in Mount Ephraim: and the children of Israel came up to her for judgment (Judges 4:4-5). Some consider it unexpected for God to raise up a woman as prophetess. But the New Testament makes it clear that God grants the gift of prophecy unto women also, and they are to practice it appropriately (1 Corinthians 11:5). From 1 Corinthians 11:5, we find that the essential element to a woman's ministry as a prophetess in the early church was her obvious submission to the male leadership in the church (evidenced by her wearing of a veil). A woman was to use her gifts in the context of order established by the leaders of the church - just like anyone's gift.

Deborah also judged Israel at that time, and the children of Israel came up to her for judgment. Often it is assumed that Deborah was allowed leadership because men failed to take the position. While later, we will see that Barak doesn't seem to be all he should be, we have no indication that he failed to do something God told him to do in taking leadership.

Even more consider it unexpected for God to raise up a woman to be a judge - a *shaphat*, a heroic leader for Israel. Deborah was a woman greatly used by God, and she was also a woman who respected the people God put in authority over her - notably, Barak. The issue, from a New Testament perspective, is not whether women can be used greatly by God. *Of course they can.* The issue is one of headship, final accountability, and authority - and God has granted these responsibilities to men in both the home and the church. Women can be used greatly by God, but it is to be under the headship of male authority in the church.

The reasons have nothing to do with any notion of male superiority; they have to do with God's ordained order (1 Corinthians 11:3), in light of God's order of creation (1 Corinthians 11:8-9), in light of the presence of watching angels (1 Corinthians 11:10), and in light of the nature of the fall (1 Timothy 2:14). The reasons also have nothing to do with any notion of female inferiority; even as Jesus was under the headship and authority of His Father (John 5:19) without being inferior in any way (John 1:1; John10:30) (David Guzik's Commentary on the Bible Judges 4 Verses 1-24).

Anna

There was much evil then in the church, yet God left not himself without witnesses. Anna always dwelt in, or at least attended at, the temple. She was always in a praying spirit; gave herself to prayer, and in all things she served God. Those to whom Christ is made known, have great reason to thank the Lord. She taught others concerning him. Let the example of the venerable saints, Simeon and Anna, give courage to those whose hoary heads are, like theirs, a crown of glory, being found in the way of righteousness. The lips soon to be silent in the grave, should be showing forth the praises of the Redeemer. In all things it became Christ to be made like unto his brethren, therefore he passed through infancy and childhood as other children, yet without sin, and with manifest proofs of the Divine nature in him. By the Spirit of God all his faculties performed their offices in a manner not seen in any one else. Other children have foolishness bound in their hearts, which appears in what they say or do, but he was filled with wisdom, by the influence of the Holy Ghost; everything he said and did, was wisely said and wisely done, above his years. Other children show the corruption of their nature; nothing but the grace of God was upon him (Lu 2:41-52) (Luke 2- Matthew Henry's Concise Commentary on the Bible).

Rahab

Rahab had heard of the miracles the Lord wrought for Israel. She believed that his promises would certainly be fulfilled, and his threatenings take effect; and that there was no way of escape but by submitting to him, and joining with his people. The conduct of Rahab proved that she had the real principle of Divine faith. Observe the promises the spies made to her. The goodness of God is often expressed by his kindness and truth, Ps 117:2; in both these we must be followers of him. Those who will be conscientious in keeping promises, are cautious in making them. The spies make needful conditions. The scarlet cord, like the blood upon the doorpost at the passover, recalls to remembrance the sinner's security under the atoning blood of Christ; and that we are to flee thereto for refuge from the wrath of a justly offended God. The same cord Rahab used for the saving of these Israelites was to be used for her own safety. What we serve and honor God with, we may expect he will bless, and make useful to us (Joshua 2:22-24) (Joshua 2- Matthew Henry's Concise Commentary on the Bible).

These three examples show us how to honor God with our words, our actions, and our bodies. Our loyalty must be to God at all times. If it did not begin there, we should ensure it ends there.

6

Ultimate Respect
(For Self and Others)

As we prepare to close out our discussion on the power women were given by God and His purpose for woman, we must address one final topic: respect. Now that we know the woman was uniquely created by God, the struggles they have been through in the days of the Bible and within the United States for the last few centuries, how to be faithful over the use of our gifts, how to highly esteem our sisters, and how to be a vessel of honor, we can discuss having respect for ourselves and others.

When people have been mistreated over a period of time, they have a tendency to expect nothing less than what they have been getting. For example, if a child is accustomed to getting spankings, he/she will have a tendency to flinch when the parent raises his/her hand. This is also true for women who are beaten by their spouses. If a person is frequently around people who curse or have rude behavior, he/she will develop like tendencies. Negative behaviors can cause people to lack self-respect if they buy into the concept of being worthless. However, God does not require that we respect ourselves any less due to our past experiences.

Over the course of time, there has been a breakdown in the family unit, and many fathers have not been living in the home to assist in raising the children. At one time, women were primarily homemakers, so they could stay home and raise the children. However, with the men not being in the home and offering full financial support, mothers have been forced into the workplace. Women often times fulfill the roles of both mother and father, and they become the breadwinners. With the added responsibility that women take on, they also become the decision maker and head of the household. This causes women to have an overall lack of respect for men, and it shows in the way they speak to them. Women have been known to speak loudly to men, in an attempt to over talk them and to show the men they are self sufficient. This apparent disdain for men has grown from past and present experiences. However, this lack of respect toward men does not line up with the word of God.

In other situations, women who seemingly have it all together have a tendency to look down on other women who may have made bad decisions that have adversely affected their lives. Anyone at any time can go down the wrong path by making one bad decision. They do not realize one day it could be them or it could have been them when they made bad choices. Rather than realizing how truly blessed they are to be in God's arc of safety, they have a tendency to see their successes to be due to their own strength. This lack of respect for other women is unacceptable.

Regardless of what a person has done, we should try to see him/her as God sees him/her. The word of God tells us to love our neighbors and to give honor where honor is due. We may not like what a person represents or what they have done to us, but when we disrespect them, we in turn disrespect our creator and ourselves.

To improve your viewpoint about yourself and others, read the word of God to learn the proper treatment of self and others. There are two lists of scriptures that follow. The first list of scripture tells us about having respect for others. The second list tells us about having self-respect. If you find yourself challenged in this area, meditate day and night on the word of God. The word of God is life changing. Remember, we want to do what God commands us to do and be who He has called us to be in all we do!

Scriptures on Respecting Others

James 2:9
But if you show partiality, you are committing sin and are convicted by the law as transgressors.

Romans 13:7
Render to all what is due them: tax to whom tax is due; custom to whom custom; fear to whom fear; honor to whom honor.

Romans 12:10
Be devoted to one another in brotherly love; give preference to one another in honor;

Philippians 2:3
Do nothing from selfishness or empty conceit, but with humility of mind let each of you regard one another as more important than himself;

2 Corinthians 10:12-16
For we are not bold to class or compare ourselves with some of those who commend themselves; but when they measure themselves by themselves, and compare themselves with themselves, they are without understanding. But we will not

boast beyond our measure, but within the measure of the sphere which God apportioned to us as a measure, to reach even as far as you. For we are not overextending ourselves, as if we did not reach to you, for we were the first to come even as far as you in the gospel of Christ; not boasting beyond our measure, that is, in other men's labors, but with the hope that as your faith grows, we shall be, within our sphere, enlarged even more by you, so as to preach the gospel even to the regions beyond you, and not to boast in what has been accomplished in the sphere of another.

Acts 10:34-35

And opening his mouth, Peter said: "I most certainly understand now that God is not one to show partiality, but in every nation the man who fears Him and does what is right, is welcome to Him.

Matthew 7:12

"Therefore, however you want people to treat you, so treat them, for this is the Law and the Prophets.

1 Peter 2:17

Honor all men; love the brotherhood, fear God, honor the king.

Hebrews 13:17

Obey your leaders, and submit to them; for they keep watch over your souls, as those who will give an account. Let them do this with joy and not with grief, for this would be unprofitable for you.

Scriptures on Self-Respect

1 Corinthians 6:20 ESV

For you were bought with a price. So glorify God in your body.

Romans 12:2 ESV

Do not be conformed to this world, but be transformed by the renewal of your mind, that by testing you may discern what is the will of God, what is good and acceptable and perfect.

2 Timothy 2:15 ESV

Do your best to present yourself to God as one approved, a worker who has no need to be ashamed, rightly handling the word of truth.

Galatians 2:20 ESV

I have been crucified with Christ. It is no longer I who live, but Christ who lives in me. And the life I now live in the flesh I live by faith in the Son of God, who loved me and gave himself for me.

Proverbs 17:22 ESV

A joyful heart is good medicine, but a crushed spirit dries up the bones.

1 Timothy 4:12-14 ESV

Let no one despise you for your youth, but set the believers an example in speech, in conduct, in love, in faith, in purity. Until I come, devote yourself to the public reading of Scripture, to exhortation, to teaching. Do not neglect the gift you have, which was given you by prophecy when the council of elders laid their hands on you.

1 John 5:4 ESV

For everyone who has been born of God overcomes the world. And this is the victory that has overcome the world— our faith.

2 Timothy 2:22 ESV

So flee youthful passions and pursue righteousness, faith, love, and peace, along with those who call on the Lord from a pure heart.

2 Corinthians 5:17 ESV

Therefore, if anyone is in Christ, he is a new creation. The old has passed away; behold, the new has come.

1 Peter 2:5 ESV

You yourselves like living stones are being built up as a spiritual house, to be a holy priesthood, to offer spiritual sacrifices acceptable to God through Jesus Christ.

2 Corinthians 12:10 ESV

For the sake of Christ, then, I am content with weaknesses, insults, hardships, persecutions, and calamities. For when I am weak, then I am strong.

Hebrews 11:6 ESV

And without faith it is impossible to please him, for whoever would draw near to God must believe that he exists and that he rewards those who seek him.

1 Corinthians 13:4 ESV

Love is patient and kind; love does not envy or boast; it is not arrogant.

Psalm 56:2-7 ESV

My enemies trample on me all day long, for many attack me proudly. When I am afraid, I put my trust in you. In God, whose word I praise, in God I trust; I shall not be afraid. What can flesh do to me? All day long they injure my cause; all their thoughts are against me for evil. They stir up strife, they lurk; they watch my steps, as they have waited for my life. ...

Jeremiah 1:5 ESV

"Before I formed you in the womb I knew you, and before you were born I consecrated you; I appointed you a prophet to the nations."

7

A Closing Thought

Prayerfully, you have been truly enlightened on God's perspective of women, their worth, and responsibilities in this earthly realm. Women were not designed to take a back seat and be treated as inferior. Women, you will be held accountable for how you choose to use your God-given talents. You will be required to give God an answer about how responsible you were and how you respected yourself and others. Be a sweet smelling savor unto our heavenly father. Be kind to yourself and to others. Lift your sisters up and show them genuine love. Remember, God created you in His image and positioned you just a little lower than the angels.

May you be blessed each and every day!

References

Archer, Dale M.D. (2013). Reading Between the (Head)Lines Human Trafficking In America.

bible.cc.com (various Bible versions).

biblegateway.com (various Bible versions).

biblehub.com. Jubilee Bible 2000.

Jackson, Wayne (n.d.) Christian Courier.

www.christiancourier.com

Tyndale House Publishers. (1996, 2004). Life Application Study Bible. Holy Bible, New Living Translation.

Women's International Center. *Women's History in America. Excerpted from Compton's Interactive Encyclopedia Copyright (c) 1994, 1995 Compton's New Media, Inc.*

Zondervan (1994, 2003). Quest Study Bible. The Holy Bible, New International Version.

Gift of Salvation for Non-Believers

"For all have sinned, and come short of the glory of God."
Romans 3:23

This section was written especially for non-believers, those who have not accepted the gift of salvation. The gift of salvation saves souls from eternal damnation and is a free gift offered by God himself. John 3:16-18 says, *"For God so loved the world, that he gave his only begotten Son, that whosoever believeth in him should not perish, but have everlasting life. For God sent not his Son into the world to condemn the world; but that the world through him might be saved. He that believeth on him is not condemned: but he that believeth not is condemned already, because he hath not believed in the name of the only begotten Son of God."* This section of scripture tells us God's purpose for giving His son Jesus to the world. The world was in a bad condition. The world was overwrought with sin; the people were living for fleshly desires rather than for God's desires.

As a result of the world's conditions, God decided that He would offer the perfect sacrifice that would save the world from being a place where people were lost and had no hope. He decided that His own son could stand in proxy for the sin-filled world, taking all sin upon Himself.

So Jesus came, born of a virgin, to save this dying world. He walked on this earth for 33 ½ years, doing the work of His Heavenly Father. At the appointed time, He died by way of crucifixion upon a cross at Calvary, on Golgatha's hill. He shed his blood and died for you and for me. Because His blood was pure, it paid the penalty for all unrighteousness and gave those who believe in Him direct access to His father's throne.

Scripture tells us in Matthew 27:51 that the veil of the temple was ripped in two from top to bottom, at the moment that Jesus' spirit left His body. As a result of the veil's removal, we are no longer required to have a high priest make intercession for us. We, as the children of the Most High God, are able to approach the throne God for ourselves, and Jesus sits on the right hand of the Father making intercession for us.

But what is even more miraculous than God offering His own son as the perfect sacrifice was the fact that when Jesus was placed in grave clothes and placed in a tomb, He only remained there until the third day. God would not have it that His son would remain in the heart of the earth forever. In order for people to believe in the awesome power of God and His dear son Jesus, a miracle had to be performed. So, on the third day, after Jesus died on the cross, He was resurrected, demonstrating the omnipotence of God. This very act was the act that would cause people to believe in a god that reigns supreme and holds the power of the universe in His very hands, a god that could save them from themselves.

Today, if you are an unbeliever, you can change your destiny. You can change where you will spend your eternity. Our Heavenly Father gives us the freedom of choice about how we want to live our life here on earth and how we want to spend eternity. In Deuteronomy 30:19, God boldly declares, "*I call heaven and earth to record this day against you, that I have set before you life and death, blessing and cursing: therefore choose life, that both thou and thy seed may live.*"

So, dear friend what choice will you make today? Will you spend your eternity with the Creator or will you suffer Hell's eternal flames? Again, the choice is yours. Just as the men aboard the ship who were with Jonah became believers, you too can make a choice to accept the only one and true living God as your god.

If after reading the above passages, you have decided that you want to spend your eternity in Heaven with God, the creator, and His son Jesus, and the Holy Spirit, read through what has affectionately come to be known as the Roman's Road. This is the road to salvation. As you read through the scriptures that comprise the Roman's Road, you will also read the explanation for each scripture so you will have clarity about what you are reading and confessing.

The Roman's Road to Salvation

The road to salvation begins with Romans 3:23 which declares, *"For all have sinned, and come short of the glory of God."* This scripture explains that everyone has come short of God's glory and needs redemption. Then Romans 6:23a states, *"For the wages of sin is death."* Here, we learn that the consequence of living a life of sin is death. Everyone will experience physical death as a result of the sin committed in the garden of Eden, but those who commit themselves to a life of sin will suffer eternal damnation in the lake of fire (Rev. 19).

Continue with the rest of verse 6:23 that says, *"but the gift of God is eternal life through Jesus Christ our Lord."* There is an alternative to suffering eternal damnation. We can accept the gift of salvation by accepting Jesus as our personal lord and savior. Then, Romans 5:8 says, *"But God commendeth his love toward us, in that, while we were yet sinners, Christ died for us."* We are able to receive the gift of salvation because Christ came to earth and shed His blood for us on the cross.

Continue to Romans 10: 9-10 which says, *"That if thou shalt confess with thy mouth the Lord Jesus, and shalt believe in thine heart that God hath raised him from the dead, thou shalt be saved. For with the heart man believeth unto righteousness; and with the mouth confession is made unto salvation."* If we confess with our mouths that Jesus is the son of God, that he came and died for our sins, and that God raised Him from the dead, we will receive salvation.

Finish with Romans 10:13, which states, *"For whosoever shall call upon the name of the Lord shall be saved."* Call upon the name of God by saying these words, **"Lord Jesus, come into my heart and save me Lord. I believe that you are the Son of God who came and died on the cross for my sins. I believe that you rose from the grave. I also believe that you now sit in heaven on the right side of the Father, making intersession for me. I accept you as my Lord and my Savior."**

Now that you have confessed with your mouth that Jesus is the son of God and that He died for our sins and rose from the grave, **YOU ARE NOW SAVED!!!!** You will spend your eternity in heaven.

The next step is very important- you must find a bible-based church that teaches the word of God and confesses the Lord Jesus Christ to be the son of God. Don't delay. Do this immediately. Do not leave yourself open to the enemy. Get connected with the saints of the Most High God and keep yourself covered with the unspotted blood of the lamb.
Here is my prayer for you.

Father God,

I thank you for the opportunity to minister your word to the unsaved, the unchurched, and the uncommitted. Father God, I pray now for the souls who have just received the gift of salvation. Lord Father, they have opened their hearts to you, and I know that you have received them into your kingdom and written their names in the Book of Life. Father God, I pray that you will touch their lives and show yourself mightily before them. Let their eyes be opened by the scales falling off, allowing them to see clearly.

Father God, I even pray for the backslider, those who have turned away from you after receiving the gift of salvation. You said in your word that you desire that none would perish. So Lord, I send your word to them right now praying that they would confess the iniquity in their heart, repent, and turn from their evil ways, so that they may receive a life of abundance. You said in your word in Matthew Chapter 14, that every knee shall bow before you and every tongue will confess that Jesus is Lord.

Father God, I pray now that we all come under subjection to your word and that we will humbly submit our lives to you. I ask all these things in the name of my Lord and Savior Jesus Christ.
Amen, Amen, Amen!!!!

I will continue to pray for your success in your walk with God. Remember, this spiritual walk that you are about to embark on will not be an easy walk, but remember, the race is not given to the swift but to those who endure to the end.

Be blessed with heaven's best. I love you!

ABOUT THE AUTHOR

Dr. Cassundra White-Elliott resides in California with her family, where as an English/Education professor she works for various community colleges and universities. One of the universities she teaches for is the Southern California Branch of the University of Phoenix. There she teaches communication studies.

When writing, she writes with the direction of the Holy Spirit, in an effort to share with God's people all that He has for them.

In addition to teaching and writing, Dr. White-Elliott also serves as an evangelistic teacher. She is also the founder of International Women's Commission, a ministry that serves the needs of the entire person, by attending to healing the mind, body, soul, and spirit.

Dr. White-Elliott holds a Ph.D. in Education, a Master's in English Composition, and a Bachelor's in Education.

Dr. White-Elliott is also the founder of CLF Publishing, LLC. For your publishing needs, go online to www.clfpublishing.org.

OTHER BOOKS BY THE AUTHOR

(All books can be purchased at www.creativemindsbookstore.com)

From Despair, through Determination, to Victory!

A lot can happen during a span of 40 years. The life of Dr. Cassundra White-Elliott has been anything but uneventful. From a fun-loving childhood sprinkled with incidents of abuse to a tumultuous young adulthood to a stable, secure adult life, she has experienced a full life, with much more to come. Her story is inspiring and motivating.

If anyone lacks hope, reading Dr. White-Elliott's autobiography will propel him/her into an attitude of "Maybe I can." This attitude, if nurtured and developed, will grow into an attitude of "Yes, I can." Throughout her life, Cassundra has always held in her heart the belief that she could achieve anything that she had a made-up mind to embark upon. She was determined to achieve her heart's desires, doing what God has called her to do. She takes no credit for herself. All the glory goes to God, for He is her driving force. In Him, she lives, moves, and has her being.

Through the Storm

Through the Storm was duly inspired by the avaricious cloud of depression that decided to hover overhead of my daily existence in the latter part of 2007. Although I found it extremely difficult, I was once again compelled to not be defeated by just another snare that the enemy, the trickster, set for me. Once again, or more appropriately I should say *continuously*, he has exerted pernicious efforts to snatch the very life out of me by causing me to wallow in despair and to believe that I had been overcome by failure when in actuality and all reality, I was just experiencing a temporary setback. During those cloudy days, I had to remind myself daily that even though I was a target of the enemy, I am and will always be a child of the Most High god, Jehovah, who is my rock, my stability.

Unleashed Anger, Anger Unleashed

Preview

Introduction

What Is This Book All About?

As I prepared to embark upon the adventure of writing this book, I had to prepare myself to also be transparent. I have found that being transparent is required in order for healing to transpire, healing for all those that peruse the pages of this book and myself. And I may as well tell you that today, at the onset of this project, I have not been totally delivered from my condition of being an anger-filled person. However, I am definitely a work in progress. I have made strides with the assistance of my Lord and Savior, Jesus Christ, who is the head of my life. Without his love, guidance, and teachings, I would not be the woman of God I am today. I shudder to think where I could be instead and will therefore not entertain the thought.

Public Speaking in the Spiritual Arena

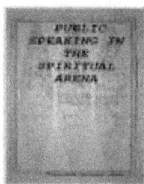

Preview

Chapter Two

How Communication Works

Purpose: This chapter will explain the six primary components of communication, identifying their purpose and how they work together.

The Source

In oral communication, the source of information is the speaker. In a church setting, the foundation of the message is God's word, but it is a speaker's interpretation of God's word that is delivered to the audience. As speakers vary, the information may vary but should have a similar essence because the foundational text is the same.

The Message

The message is the collective set of ideas that the speaker (the source) wants to deliver and/or illustrate to the audience. The message can be informative where the speaker informs the audience about a specific set of information. Or, the message may be persuasive in nature if the speaker wants to persuade the audience about conducting themselves in a specific manner, accepting God's commandments, or any number of things.

Where is Your Joppa?

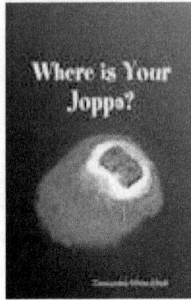

Introduction

Where is Your Joppa? was written for the express purpose of illustrating God's call for obedience in the lives of believers with respect to the individual call that He has on each of our lives. As you read throughout the various chapters, notice that the emphasis is placed on our persistent disobedience in answering God's call in a specific area of our lives. We have become a people who are similar to the Israelites when they found themselves in the middle of the wilderness, following their exodus from Egypt. Before God, they murmured and complained about their current life conditions and failed to be obedient to God's statutes delivered through His servant Moses. Their persistent disobedience caused them to lose the opportunity to see and enter the Promised Land. I ask you, "What has your disobedience cost you?" "Was your disobedience worth what it cost you?" "Do you think about the souls you could have ushered into the kingdom of God?" These are some of the questions that I pray will be answered through your reading of the book.

Mayhem in the Hamptons

Romero and Yolanda optimistically plan for the day that is going to change their lives from being single persons to a couple who is united in holy matrimony. They, along with their parents, close friends and family, fly over to the infamous Hamptons, where only the rich and famous vacation, to have their dream wedding at the five-star Hampton Suites located on a peninsula in the Hamptons. Little do they know that their perfect day will turn out to be less than perfect when their wedding planner Mariesha Coleman suddenly goes missing!

A time when the newlyweds' lives should be filled with joy and the creation of wonderful memories, they are stricken with grief as they desperately try to find clues to help solve Mariesha's disappearance.

Mayhem in the Hamptons is a tale that shares how the horrors of a woman's past can come back to haunt her in more than one way and the impact it can have on anyone who gets in the way.

Preacher's Daughter

Tinisha, the daughter of a preacher, is a twenty-six year old God-fearing young woman endeavoring to complete law school so that she can make her mark in the courtroom. Working in one of the late-night clubs in Hollywood to earn money to pay her own way through school, Tinisha soon learns that life doesn't always go as planned. Finding her strength in her faith, Tinisha constantly finds herself praying as she watches God move miraculously in her life.

Preacher's Son

Romero Turner is a private investigator with a promising future. As he continues to build his career, he is excited about the cases he undertakes. However, his father Pastor Theodore Turner has other plans for his son's life. In the midst of trying to save his client's husband from Sylvestor Domingo, a ruthless crime lord, Romero must try to salvage his relationship with his father. He must decide if ministry or life as a detective is in his future.

Lord, Teach Me to be a Blessing!

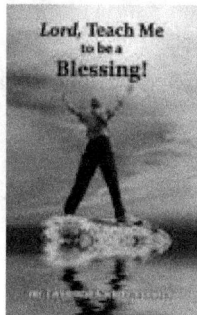

Lord, Teach Me to be a Blessing! will change a person's mentality from being centered around "me, myself, and I" to focusing on "others."

The world system teaches us that it is acceptable to place ourselves above others in an attempt to get ahead and even to survive. Herbert Spencer coined the phrase *'survival of the fittest'* after reading Charles Darwin's theory of evolution. This concept of surpassing and outdoing others is the world's philosophy.

However, the word of God does not subscribe to or promote this self-centered ideology, and therefore, neither should believers. We must hold fast to the truths outlined in Holy Scripture: *"Love thy neighbor as you love thyself"* (James 2:8) and *"It is more blessed to give than to receive"* (Acts 20:35). While holding God's truths to be self evident, we must demonstrate them to others, thereby showing them the way of the Lord of how to be a blessing to someone *rather* than looking to receive a blessing.

This is the very purpose of this book: to change the mentality of the world from being *self* centered to *other* centered.

After the Dust Settles

Throughout the journey of life, we all experience ups and downs and joys and pains. Most of us successfully find solutions to the situations/problems we encounter, but we often avoid dealing with the attached emotions. If we continue to ignore the emotions of pain, hurt, disappointment, anger, etc., we set ourselves up for destruction. Our families, our cultures, and our society tell us to be strong, to keep our chin up, and to grin and bear it. However, these methods of avoidance can lead us to strokes due to the undue amount of pressure we place on ourselves and/or mental illness from being unable to cope with the emotional baggage we have accumulated.

In *After the Dust Settles,* Dr. C. White-Elliott shares several situations that we all may encounter at one time or another in our lifetime and how to successfully navigate through them, so we can find ourselves emotionally healthy after the dust has settled and the situation has been rectified.

Begin reading today and experience a better tomorrow!